WHO WANTS WATERMELON FOR BREAKFAST?

Business lessons to profit your everyday life

ALICIA D. RITCHEY, Ed.D.

© 2023 ALICIA RITCHEY, Ed.D.
WHO WANTS WATERMELON FOR BREAKFAST?

All rights reserved. No part of this publication may be reproduced, stored in a retrieval system or transmitted in any form or by any means, electronic, mechanical, photocopying, recording or otherwise without the prior permission of the publisher or in accordance with the provisions of the Copyright, Designs and Patents Act 1988 or under the terms of any license permitting limited copying issued by the Copyright Licensing Agency. For permission requests, write to the copyright holder at aritch@aritchenterprise.com, and use the subject line: Permission to Reproduce. Address your request "Attention: Permission to Reproduce "Who Wants Watermelon for Breakfast?" book.

Published by:
INDIGOLIFE COMMUNICATIONS, INC.
www.indigolifeonline.com
admin@indigolifeonline.com
800.844.7139

Editors:
Linda Barnes, MBA
Sharon Samuels, Ed.D.
Wendy Wilson, Ed.D.

CONTACT AUTHOR:
Dr. Alicia Ritchey
aritch@aritchenterprise.com
www.aritchenterprise.com

ISBN-13: 979-8-9879270-0-7

DISCLAIMER

The stories shared in this book are based on the personal life experiences of the author and others. The author uses the stories to provide entertainment and inspiration, and to provide examples that illustrate and clarify the points made about business and life. The stories and experience are not intended to be taken as professional, legal, or financial advice. The author and publisher make no representations, stated or implied, about the completeness, accuracy, reliability, suitability, or availability of any information presented in this book, for any purpose. Readers are advised to consult with a qualified legal, business, or financial professional before making any decisions based on the information presented in this book. The reader assumes all risks with any use of this book and the information presented therein.

The author makes no assurance as to any financial outcome based on the use of the book. The author and publisher shall not be held liable for any losses or damages that may arise from the use of the information presented in this book. This includes, but is not limited to, any direct or indirect damages, incidental damages, special damages, or consequential damages resulting from the use of this book, or any information contained within it.

By reading this book, the reader agrees to hold harmless the author and publisher from any claims or damages arising from the use of information presented in this book. The reader also agrees to indemnify the author and publisher against any claims or damages arising from the use of information presented in this book by any third party.

No Consultant-Client Privilege

The author is a business consultant. However, reading this book does not create a consultant-client relationship between the reader and the author. Absent an agreement to the contrary, the author is not a consultant to the reader. This book is for educational purposes only.

DEDICATION

This book is dedicated to my mother, Ozzie Ritchey Palmer. Thank you, Mother. You embody the watermelon symbolized in this text. Your love and wisdom have fed countless others, and your seeds will continue to bear fruit throughout generations.

CONTENTS

FOREWORD	Dr. Sheva Quinn..	i
SLICE 1	Who Wants Watermelon for Breakfast?........	1
SLICE 2	In Your Lane..	5
SLICE 3	I Got the Power...	15
SLICE 4	Let the Social Worker Get By: Packaged for the Front of the Line...............	23
SLICE 5	Are You Generating Revenue or Wealth?.....	29
SLICE 6	Products or Services: Where does the Money Reside?....................	37
SLICE 7	Return of the Revolution.............................	45
SLICE 8	Shhh… The Termites are Speaking..............	51
SLICE 9	Pitching to the Right Client.........................	59
SLICE 10	No Golfing inside the Warehouse................	67
SLICE 11	Opportunity out of Crisis............................	75
SLICE 12	Preparing for Time and Chance...................	83
SLICE 13	Share the Gift. Walk In Purpose..................	91
SLICE 14	Get Your own Dictionary!............................	103

FOREWORD

Who remembers the watermelon truck?

If you are from the South, then you should know all about the watermelon business.

Hailed from Africa, and seeds transported through the trans-atlantic slave trade, the watermelon was known as the profit fruit to Black farmers. Before it was devalued and used to dehumanize Black people, watermelon was, in fact, the most sought-after fruit in America. After slavery ended, 1865-1867, Black farmers used watermelon farming to sustain their families and to generate wealth.

What happened, you may ask?

As a result of the societal climate, specifically in the South, the economic progress among Black people was stymied due to a shift from the watermelon being a commodity to later becoming a symbol of shame and disdain. The watermelon started to be used in black-face cartoons to employ racial mockery and to create a dislike for the fruit, resulting in plummeting sales for Black farmers.

Blacks farmers yet found a way to continue to grow profits while keeping their heritage and culture alive. As seen today, many Black growers are still thriving off watermelon seeds that were planted in their families. In addition to generating wealth in the Black community, the watermelon enabled Black relatives to connect with distant family members and their ancestors. For Black people, the harvesting of watermelons symbolized the beginning of summer and family reunions! And no family reunion was ever complete without fresh cut slices of watermelon.

Like a good watermelon, this book is ripe with many business principles and strategies that can help transform and sweeten your personal and professional life.

Each Slice is a delicious and fulfilling experience of wisdom, insight, and thoughtful perspective. Be sure to sow the seeds as you prepare to harvest a wealth of fruit for you and your legacy.

Now on to Watermelon PROFITS!

Sheva Quinn, Ed.D.
Black Classical University, Black History Professor

INTRODUCTION

SLICE 1

WHO WANTS WATERMELON FOR BREAKFAST?

During the COVID-19 Pandemic, it occurred to me that this is the season for the ***have-nots***. While we each have something in our possession; when compared to big boy mainstream corporations, what we have may not look like much. Despite their great possessions, it is mainstream corporations that we hear of now closing their doors, calling it quits, and taking flight. Why is that? Could it be that they panic at the threat of losing everything, and to be left with 'nothing.'

Ha! Nothing?! That's always been the story of the little man, those with meager means. You talk to your grandparents, your parents, your uncles, your aunts, and they will tell you that in our community, we've never been afraid of having 'nothing.' Being at the bottom of the barrel, having to skim from the crumbs of 'nothing,' was the only reality for many. Truth is, the same 'nothing' was always enough. It was just what we needed. It did not matter what were the times, whether times of plenty or seeming lack, we knew how to take that crock full of 'nothing' and make something wonderful out of it. We not only survived, but we also thrived. We were thriving in that we found ways to feed our families, ways to support our children when they went off to college. We found ways to start businesses. And, we did this supposedly with 'nothing'. As a community, said to be the **have-nots**, we have never been the ones to run from 'nothing'. So, I say again, this is our season, and if you would just get something in your hand, you can make it! You can feed, not just your family; you can feed an entire community.

Now back to the topic at hand, "Who wants watermelon for breakfast?" Ironically, I live in Cordele, Georgia, said to be the Watermelon Capital of the world. The question or topic is taken from an instance in my childhood when my siblings and I were much younger. My Dad was working for himself as a painting contractor. At the time, work was very slow due to the rainy season, which made it non-conducive for outdoor painting. With hardly any work, there was a financial strain on our household since my dad was the major bread winner in the family. During this period, my mother felt compelled to step in as a greater financial contributor to help meet the needs of the household, comprised of a family of ten, with my youngest sister not yet born.

One morning, as the eight children gathered for breakfast, it appeared that we would have to go hungry, seeing as there was hardly any food to prepare a meal. With ten mouths to feed,

Mother pondered, "Where will we get the food to feed these eight children plus myself and my husband?" She looked over to the counter and there sat 'nothing.' This 'nothing' was in the form of a watermelon. It was nothing alright. Like many who had been in situations of lack, this 'nothing' was all that Mama needed. Being the wise woman that she is, in a melodic tone, she bellowed out, "Who wants watermelon for breakfast?" My siblings and I looked at each other as if to ask, "Did she say watermelon?" We did not interpret it as a mere watermelon. Having watermelon for breakfast meant we could start the day enjoying our favorite ingredient—sugar. We were familiar with eggs for breakfast. We knew grits, sausage, and bacon for breakfast, but that day it was sugar! So, with excitement, we exclaimed in unison, "We doooooooo."

Imagine that! What others may define as 'nothing,' Mama took it, added swag to it, and sold it to an entire team. So, who wanted watermelon for breakfast? We did. Mama sliced that sugar baby into pieces right down to the rind too, and got out of it as much as she could, leaving not one disgruntled player on the team. She essentially took 'nothing,' packaged it with hoopla and made a sale. We bought it, and we were full and satisfied.

How does this relate to you as a budding entrepreneur, who may think of yourself as a 'have-not' in areas of your business? Well, you have something—something that others may call 'nothing.' However, if you take it and do with it as Mama did, engulf it with all the swag you can muster, then you can distribute it and sell it to the masses knowing that many are hungry and ready to buy what you possess.

So, ask yourself, what's stopping you from selling what's in your hand? Perhaps you haven't seen the value of it. Perhaps all you need is a convincing pitch and a melodic tone. Maybe, you need a strategy for advertising and marketing, or a system to automate your process. Whatever you need to get your offering into the marketplace, do not be convinced that there is no worth in what sits on your counter, or better said, what's in your hand. Instead, know that there is a consumer waiting to experience your innovation. After all, watermelon for breakfast is a novel idea. ***Take a bite! Enjoy the Slice!***

SLICE 2

IN YOUR LANE.

One day, I received a text from two of my sister-friends. The text was a photo of a beautiful arrangement of gourmet cookies they had baked and boxed for shipment. Their text reminded me of another sister-friend, who is also an amazing creative interior designer. I was on a roll, just thinking of all the women I knew who are great designers in their respective fields: floral arrangements, knitting, t-shirt designs, and shoe embellishments, to name a few. I thought to myself, "God, I wish I could design something … anything."

Then it occurred to me that I am a creative designer also; I design with words, a verbal architect, you might say. In that moment, it became even more clear to me how I use words and wrap them around ideas to help others design strategies, articulate their missions and visions, and communicate value for their personal and business brands. Even though I had been honing my writing skills for decades, I never connected my writing to an expression of creative design. Since then, I embrace my gift as a designer. In fact, as a way of publicly acknowledging my creativity, I make it a point to affix the word 'designer' to my business title; hence, the reference to myself as a ***strategic business designer.***

A year or so after having this epiphany, I took a scroll through one of the Facebook groups of which I am a member. In the group, I saw a woman who shared a live video. She described herself as a business builder. As I listened to all the strategies she discussed, I thought about the title I had given to myself, "***strategic business designer***" and pondered whether I could live up to its meaning.

It was clear that I did not have the vast knowledge possessed by the woman on the Facebook live video. I considered whether I should just give up my title. Obviously, the crown and sash belonged to her, right? To make things worse, I visited her website, and I really started to feel intimidated. I mean she is a boss chick for real. I went from simply admiring what she does to questioning whether I could deliver on my own promise. Since I am not a business builder, and her knowledge base far exceeded mine, shouldn't I just pack my bags and go home? Guess what? Just as loudly and boldly as the voice of an imposter would have me second guess my value, my gifts and talents, my capacity, and my preparedness, another voice spoke to me and said, "No, you're not a business builder! You are a business designer! There is a difference. Now stay in your lane! You are intimidated by her because you are in her lane, not yours. Reverse and go around. Realign yourself!"

The voice continued to drive home the point: ***"The only time you need to be intimidated is when you are in lanes you do not need to be!"***

Here I was over there with the general contractor and the construction workers—the builders; however, my job was to be the architect and engineer—the designer. What would I look like with a hammer and a nail in hand trying to build, when all I'm to do is draft the blueprint with words? While the woman was great as the builder, it is possible that she may not be as great as a designer, and certainly not with the same uniqueness and expression as I. Just as I could not build like she does, she perhaps could not design like I do.

From that experience, I discovered some amazing seeds that are useful to help propel growth. Before planting the seeds, start by asking yourself, "In what areas of my life, if any, am I feeling intimidated?" Also ask yourself, "Where am I? And am I supposed to be here? Is this my lane?" If you can identify where you are, and if you can answer emphatically that you are supposed to be there, then you do not need to be intimidated by anyone else. Once again, your lane is the space and opportunity that is purposed for you to uniquely exercise your gifts, in a way that no one else, but you can.

I should share that throughout the following discussion, I use the example of a highway to help explain what it means to be in your lane. When thinking about a highway, we can describe this as the overall sector or career field you occupy. If you are a business owner, you might think of the highway as the general industry of your business. As for how we define your lane, this may be the specific product or service that you offer. It may also be a unique method that you use to deliver your product or service to your clientele. You can also define your lane as your company's vision, mission, and philosophical statement. So, you see, the highway is general, and your lane is specific to you, your business, and your purpose.

ALICIA D. RITCHEY, Ed.D.

In a sea of businesses, your company can easily get lost and overlooked for opportunities. Therefore, it is not enough to know your industry (highway) and the product/service that you offer (your lane); you also must understand and be able to articulate how your lane functions as a major contribution to the sustainability of the whole highway—part of an economic development system to transport people within and across communities. Otherwise, what you offer may be viewed and dismissed as insignificant, having no value. Now on to our three seeds.

1st Seed: Study the highway to stay in your lane.

Let us start by understanding that the phrase 'stay in your lane' is not an arbitrary directive. There is a lot to unpack around this phrase, and when we take it on as a serious exercise, we sharpen our business acumen, and increase our chances for entrepreneurial success. While great emphasis is placed on staying in your lane, we cannot disregard the importance of knowing the highway, as well. After all, to stay in your lane, you have to understand the role your lane plays as a part of the entire highway. Therefore, it is critically important to have a general knowledge of the highway itself. When you know the highway, you have a level of insight and clarity about major aspects of the journey and the road you are travelling. You know your starting point. In a business sense, this means you know where your business is located—you know the industry category of your products and services; and you can speak the language of that sector. You are aware of industry standards, and you remain abreast of updates made to technology and systems.

Additionally, you are familiar with best practices used to mitigate risks and maintain efficiency, as well as increase productivity.

Knowing the highway also means that you understand the amenities and requirements of that roadway, in comparison to another route of travel. You have an idea of whether this is the best way to get to your destination since each highway has significant differences. As we know, some highways give you scenery and quaint shops along nearby exits. Other highways might be a faster route to your destination, saving you travel time. For example, if I am traveling to Cordele, Georgia from Miami, Florida, there are at least two ways to travel. I can travel the Turnpike to I-75 North. I can also take the route of I-95 North to I-10 West to I-75 North. It might take me up to an hour longer by traveling I-95 than it would take me to travel the Turnpike. While taking I-75 and the Turnpike saves me on time, it does cost me more money in tolls. On the other hand, while I-95 may offer a scenic route and save me money, it costs me more time.

Using highway travel as an analogy for where you are headed on your business journey, what are your short-term and long term goals? What predictions can you make about the time it will take for you to reach your goals? Seeing the highway that you are traveling, what is required for your safe and timely arrival to profit and success? Will it require continuing education, more credentials and acquisition of new skill sets, mentoring, coaching, additional financing, mental toughness, a business plan, etc.? Again, knowing the highway means that we are aware of what the highway gives and takes. Otherwise, we may not be prepared for travel.

ALICIA D. RITCHEY, Ed.D.

Sometimes, what makes one highway a more attractive travel route over another is the number of lanes. While the HOV lane might get you there faster than the other lanes, your comfort level may not be for fast-speed driving. Personally, on a three or four lane highway, I am more comfortable driving in the middle lane. The left lane is closest to the median, and the drivers on the outer lane travel more slowly than I would like to drive. Notice that whatever lane you drive, you may still be prompted to temporarily move to another lane. In other words, staying in your lane does not limit you to your lane only. Staying in your lane still gives you access to the entire highway. At any given moment, you can travel into other lanes as you wish or as needed. Likewise, operating in your expertise does not limit you to a single niche in your industry.

Whichever is your preferred or designated lane on the highway, what all the lanes on the highway have in common is that all their traffic flows in the same direction. However, depending on the intention of the traveler, it may be necessary to ride in a particular lane. Let's say, I want to get off at one of the Plazas along the Florida Turnpike. I would drive in the left lane since the access point to the Plazas are on the left side of the highway. If I wanted to exit the Florida Turnpike completely, I would do so from the right lane on the highway. The same goes for staying in your lane. Your lane, or what you offer in your business, runs parallel to what other business owners offer. However, there are travelers, or consumers, who can only access what they want or need by riding into your lane. That said, "How prepared are you to carry them where they need to go?"

2nd Seed: Be clear about the value of your lane and its unique role on the highway.

In the marketplace, your uniqueness might be described as product differentiation—how you stand out from everyone else. We can still use the metaphor of the multi-lane highway to consider product differentiation. Notice that the unique value you offer is not likely to be found in any other lane. In other words, with your product differentiation, you are the missing link that your competitors need. You fill a gap that adds value. Now seen in the light of a complement, you redefine your relationship with your competitor. In fact, no longer are you viewed as the competition, but rather as a partner. Again, understanding your product differentiation, you understand what makes you stand out in the crowd and the value that your lane adds to the highway.

Remember, people, including your competition, will value your business when your business helps to solve their problems. So, if you what you offer is the missing link that fulfills a specific need that your competitor has, then you have just provided a solution to some problem they have. Once I recognize that my product or service can benefit my competitor, then we don't have to work against each other for the same clientele. Instead, we can serve the same clientele in different capacities. Now everybody wins.

That said, from the position of a single lane—your lane—you are a majorly important component of the whole highway and transportation system. In fact, if you remove your lane from the highway, then it is no longer the same highway. If we establish that I-95 is a four-lane highway, and you find yourself traveling on a three-lane highway, it should be obvious to you that you are not on I-95. We cannot arbitrarily remove a lane from a highway and still maintain that this is the same travel route. This would completely confuse the travelers and disrupt the flow of traffic, causing unnecessary traffic jams and possible accidents.

Metaphorically speaking, the same principle applies when you look at the impact that your company has on the industry. Using the analogy of the lane (your company's products and services) and the highway (your industry), we can say that you cannot haphazardly remove your lane from the highway. Just as the lane is to the highway, your product or service is so important to the industry that not having you included would completely change the composition of an entire industry, leaving a void in the market.

3rd Seed: Be confident to articulate your value.

The ability to effectively communicate your value is what will give you access to the other lanes on the highway. Imagine that! You do not have to move across the whole highway to get your products and service into other lanes. Your former competitor, who is now your new partner, will help transport your products and services into other lanes. Simply stay in your lane, be a solution, and articulate your value, so that others understand that what you offer is the missing link that they need.

Going back to the example of the young lady who is the business builder; I can say to her, "Let me make your job easier. If you will allow me to help design your clients' businesses, by the time they get to you, they will be clear about what they need from you. That way, you do not have to waste time by helping your clients *design their businesses*. You can simply do what you do best, and that is to **build their businesses.**"

If I can communicate to a competitor the ways in which I can make their job easier, then my former competitor, who is now my partner, will be more likely to send their clients to me. Now I have just doubled my clientele to include those who are referred to me by the business builder. The point is, I do not need to be intimidated by who's in this lane or who's in that lane. All I need to do is understand where I'm going, stay in my lane of expertise, understand my contribution to the highway or industry, and be able to articulate my value in a way that is meaningful to those in other lanes. And guess what I just did? I accessed the entire highway from my lane. While in my lane, not only am I improving my own craft; I'm also getting better at helping other business owners serve their clients. It bears repeating, we do not need to feel intimidated unless we are operating in lanes that we do not need to be. Stay in your lane and work it, knowing that there is a skill that you have, a gift that you have, a talent that you have that no one can execute in the same way as you.

Finally, do not allow the imposter syndrome to cause you to question your proficiency and capability, although this is common, especially if we are venturing into new areas. Truth is, even for those of us who have a proven history of excellence in a particular area, self-limiting thoughts still come. What I have learned, however, is that while you cannot control what thoughts come to mind, you can control what thoughts you entertain. With these seeds, hopefully you now have the strategy to overcome any thought or idea that runs counter to your design of excellence—excellence which is most evident when you're in your lane. By understanding the lane that is yours, you know where you're best suited to drive. This means you know when to pass, slow down, give way, and wave others to go on ahead; when to detour, pivot, or course correct; and finally, when it may be time to make your exit on to bigger and better things. What are you waiting for? Let's get to driving! ***Take a bite! Enjoy the Slice!***

SLICE 3

I GOT THE POWER.

Recently, I was discussing with a friend some challenges she faced with someone who rented her Airbnb in South Florida. She called and shared with me her frustration about how the renters left her home in unfavorable conditions. They stole pillows and had a party, which was in violation of the rules in the rental agreement that clearly stated that no parties were allowed. There was evidence of alcohol in cups on the coffee table, cake icing on the floor, and more cake icing on the furniture. While she had good reason to be upset, it seemed that she would never stop venting about her losses.

After some time passed, I had had enough, and finally said to her, "Listen, you just made $750 over two days, and you're crying about a couple of $5 pillows, alcohol in cups left on the coffee table, and cake icing on the floor. If you total the perceived losses, they still do not exceed what you've gained. You need to understand that you are in the position of ownership, yet you are behaving like an employee."

This conversation reminds me of one of the greatest amenities of entrepreneurship: the power to own, and more importantly, ownership of power. Speaking of my friend, she owned the house and the business; but she failed to own her power. As an entrepreneur of your business and your life, you have power! I mean loads of power—the power to decide, the power to determine, and the power to define. You see, entrepreneurship is not just about owning a business and assets. It is more than just owning systems and a management style. It is about owning the power that you have, and how you can leverage your power to influence others to take certain action, whether to follow you on social media, to purchase a certain product or service, to tell someone else about your business, etc. In the following seeds, we explore the power we possess as entrepreneurs and the difference this makes in our business.

1st Seed: Owning your power, you decide whether you will win or whether you will lose.

Can you imagine having the power to decide whether you win or lose? Well, guess what? As an entrepreneur of your life and your business, you have that authority. It is just that simple. While the power to decide is sometimes an overlooked asset, most will agree that the quality of our lives is a matter of the decisions we make. If this is the case, we can reasonably say that our decisions include our choice to win or lose.

Granted, this requires a mindset shift around what it means to win or lose. Generally speaking, the concepts of winning and losing are often measured in numeric values. Both terms are used to describe the outcome of competition between two or more parties, where obviously, the party that wins has more points, and the party that loses has fewer points. Notice that in a competition between two parties, unless there is a tie, only one side gets to win, and the other party loses.

The great thing about entrepreneurship, however, is that the entrepreneur does not have to compete with another person or entity. Therefore, there is always the opportunity for a win, depending on the entrepreneur's ability to find the gain. As a former classroom educator, I recall that learning gains were an important measure of students' academic growth. Even though, not every student demonstrated the required mastery for grade-level promotion, some still made significant learning gains that were noted in their academic profiles. For those students, gains were a victory—an academic win.

For the entrepreneur, who has decided to win, competition is not against another person or entity. Instead, competition is personal; and winning is a matter of choice—the choice to become better today than yesterday. Simply put, winning means to allow one's gifts and talents to flow as purpose is fulfilled. To win is to show up and not give up, to manifest gains, whether the gain is in revenue, or in lessons learned. This definition of winning is applicable when the entrepreneur is operating from a growth mindset and a mode of surplus.

To the contrary, to lose is to give up; it means to miss the opportunity for personal, professional, and business growth. Giving up suggests that the entrepreneur is closed for sales and for profits, but more importantly, the entrepreneur is closed-minded. Once this happens, a glass ceiling is self-imposed and lowered because the entrepreneur operates from a mode of deficit.

So how will you use your power? What have you decided? Have you decided to win or lose? Despite the outcome of today's activities, regardless of what is in the register, the bank account, or the investment portfolio, as the entrepreneur of your business, own your power, decide to win, and identify the gains.

2nd Seed: Owning your power, you get to determine the value of your win.

If you have decided to win, the value of your win still needs to be determined. In so doing, you get to establish that the value of your win is greater than the value of your perceived loss. Let's go back to the rental experience of my friend. The focus of her attention was on what did not go well. By her own admission, she concluded her experience was a great loss; in essence, saying that the value of the loss was greater than the value of the win she desired. How absurd is that? She earned $750 in two days, yet she bickered about three $5 pillows and cake icing on the floor that could easily be cleaned with a cheap cleanser. What a waste of power and valuable resource…peace of mind!

Do the math with me. If she were to book the house for 20 days out of the month, she could potentially earn more than $7,500 each month, and more during peak seasons. Even with a similar rental experience of minimal loss, she would likely still net up to $7,000, which is substantially more than the revenue she would generate with a private rental. Not to dismiss the normal level of frustration one might feel with any degree of loss, the question remains, "Is the value of the win greater than the value of what was loss?" Often, even when the answer is "yes," people will forego their right to power by focusing solely on the loss.

In addition to monetary wins, we cannot overlook other type victories (i.e., public awareness of our brand and the establishment of goodwill, as well as client referrals and lead generations, where one client is always a lead to another). Other wins can be lessons we learn through the opportunities to improve our products and services. When we add up the value of our wins, in contrast to what appears to be a loss, we may find that our wins are of such significance, that prolonged focus on negligible losses is absurd and nonsensical.

3rd Seed: Owning your power, you can define the nature of the experience.

At the end of the day, when you take hold of your power, you also get to assess the experience in its totality. From an aerial viewpoint, you get to declare the overall experience as a victory or a defeat—understanding that victory and defeat are mutually exclusive—you, yourself, cannot experience a victory and a defeat in the same game. My friend could not move beyond the focus of what she lost. Therefore, she inevitably determined her own defeat. Her defeat was not about what transpired with the person who rented the Airbnb. Her defeat was more about how she processed the experience and did not exercise her power as owner of the business and the property.

Her defeat unfolded when she could only see three missing $5 pillows, alcohol in cups on the coffee table, and cake icing on the floor. Her focus was fixated on the losses, such that this was the entire subject of her conversation. In frustration, she displayed another negligible use of power: walking away from the overall experience having defined it as a defeat, despite the apparent wins of revenue and a favorable review by the guest, which could generate even greater earning potential.

In summary, the takeaways from the story of my friend are generalizable for purposes in our everyday lives, not only for business use. Notice that these powers work in tandem and in consecutive order—first the power to decide; followed by the power to determine, and then the power to define. Think of how different our lives would be if, when we are met with unfavorable parts of an experience, we stopped and assessed the experience from an aerial rooftop perspective. What would happen, if when we find ourselves in moments like this, we took ownership of our full rights to exercise our powers: to decide that we win, to determine that the value of our wins far exceeds the value of any perceived losses, and to define the overall experience as a victory.

The point is, when we see our experiences for the good that results from it, we are more likely to endure the journey of building sustainable empires. Additionally, we learn to convert those experiences into valuable assets that can be parlayed to amass great wealth. Consider your journey as an entrepreneur.

Think of the vast opportunities you have to own your power. Use this energy now to inspire and influence the world for greater good. **_Take a bite! Enjoy the Slice!_**

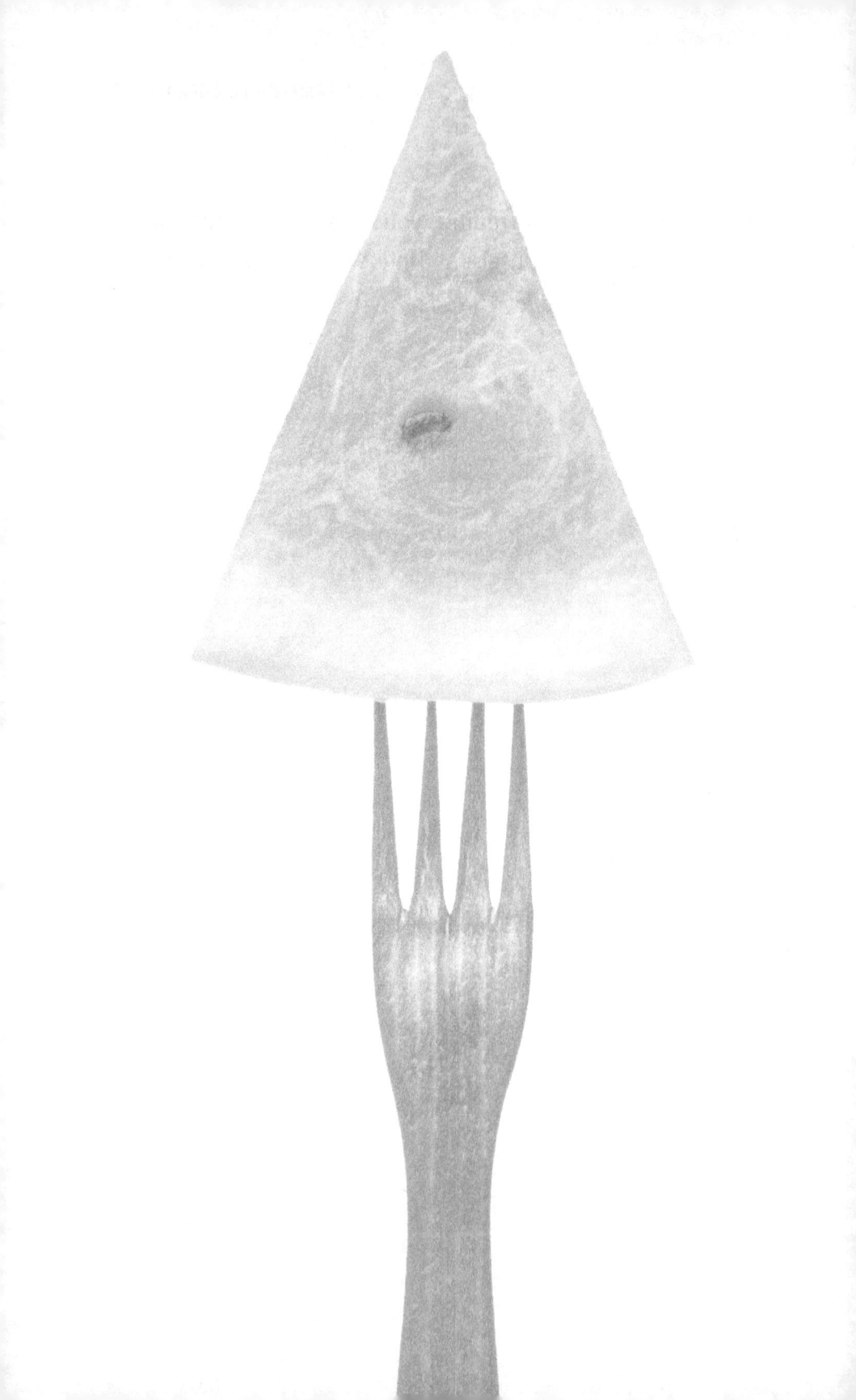

SLICE 4

LET THE SOCIAL WORKER GET BY: PACKAGED FOR THE FRONT OF THE LINE.

In Slice 1, I mentioned a period during my childhood when my Dad faced a slow season in his work. At the time, my parents only had eight children. My Mom was in college completing her bachelor's degree. Because our family needed financial support, my mother applied for food stamps. She tells the story of how she went to an agency commonly referred to as the food stamps office. While she felt uncomfortable about our family receiving food stamps, there was a serious need.

After scouting the agency, she decided that at her next visit, she did not want to stand in those long lines, waiting all day to be served. She devised a strategy to avoid the lines and to receive faster service. Noticing how the social workers were dressed, she said, "I saw them wearing pumps and their dress suits and carrying their briefcases. I said to myself, 'I'm not standing in these long lines. I'm going to dress like the social workers. That way, I can dash in and out in no time.'"

Just as she expected, when she returned to the food stamps office, she walked into the building and found that the lines were long with people waiting to be served by a case worker. Like she said she would, Mother came in wearing a dress suit with pumps and carrying a briefcase. With the curls set just right in her hair, she walked from the back of the line saying, "Excuse me, excuse me," as if she was one of the social workers trying to get to her office. While she passed people who were waiting in the long lines, other customers said to each other, "Let the social worker get by," believing that Mother was a social worker, and that the sooner she got to her office, the sooner they could receive their food stamps. Little did they know that she was a customer too, and like the other clients, Mother was also there to pick up food stamps. However, because of the way she was dressed, she was able to get to the front of the line, get her food stamps, and get to work on time. Once she made it to the window and secured her stamps, she asked the caseworker if there was a back door where she could hurriedly make her exit, without being noticed by her food stamp associates. They obliged and allowed her to leave out of the back door. She clutched her food stamps and made her escape. I'm sure we ate well after that.

There is much to draw from this experience. Stay with me as I unpack the scenario for the business lessons we can glean from Mama, the pseudo social worker.

1st Seed: Examine your packaging.

When thinking of how to package your products and services, you can learn a lot by examining ways that other companies package their goods. Look at their communication style when serving their customers, the quality of the paper they use as stationery, the boxes that contain their wares, their logos, brand colors, and brand stories—all this includes packaging—the ways in which one shows up and appears to their clientele and other stakeholders.

Examining how other companies package their goods and services provides us an opportunity to raise the value of our business brand, as well. You probably have seen advertisements for replica perfumes that might read, "If you like [that], then you'll like [this]." What the advertisers are doing is making associations with popular brands (i.e., Jimmy Choo, Chanel #5, David Yurman). They understand that when you associate an off-brand with the original, the consumer will assume both products to be of similar value. Likewise, we can gain value for our products and our services through associations with and resemblances to other high-end brands. In other words, when people see our packaging, and it reminds them of other expensive labels, then by association, it is assumed that our products and services are of comparable value. Using what we notice about how superior-ranking companies present themselves, we can then implement similar packaging strategies and techniques.

Based on the appearance of your packaging, people ascribe a certain level of value. Imagine if you were a seamstress. You sewed a wedding gown for a client, and from the looks of it, people could tell that the gown was made by an amateur seamstress. You can guess the flood of negative comments people are likely to make about the gown, not to mention the assumptions about its value. However, if the gown was styled with regal elegance, made of luxurious fabric with exotic trim and immaculate finishing, the assumption might be that the client purchased it at a premium price from an exclusive designer boutique. Even if the cost to make both gowns was the same, people would make contrasting assumptions about each product based on its presentation. The example of the two wedding gowns helps to drive home the point I am making about the appearance of packaging and the difference that packaging can make.

2nd Seed: With the right packaging, your competitors will create a pathway for you to get to the front of the line.

Remember how Mother came into the food stamps office wearing pumps and a dress suit, carrying a briefcase? The people's response to her packaging was, "Let the social worker by." They pushed back all obstacles that prevented her from getting to the front of the line. In the same way, your packaging sends messages to the public that makes an impression on even your competitors, who will then either affirm or disaffirm your value.

Therefore, depending on your packaging, your competitors, even if unknowingly, can become persuaded to speak your name in rooms and create spaces of opportunity for you. Before you know it, you will be ahead of the others who may be seeking the same opportunity as you. There it is again—your competitor can become your partner! This is a great point, especially because people sometimes view opportunity through an exclusive lens, where it's you **OR** me. Well, the 'you or me' mentality requires an unnecessary weight of performance, where you and I are relentlessly vying for the same opportunity. In this case, there is the possibility that only you or I may not get our fair share. With Mother, the competition became an ally or a resource to help her get what she wanted. There was never any competition for the food stamps since everyone would expectedly receive their due portion. Still, Mother had an agenda, to expedite the process of her being served. She devised a plan, where, despite her not being a social worker, everyone in the room esteemed her to a position of high regard, including those who stood in line, as well as the attendants at the window. Her plan was best facilitated with the right packaging, in this case, a dress suit, pumps, and a briefcase.

3rd Seed: Your packaging should be effective & efficient.

I use the word efficient with intention to draw the comparison between effective and efficient. The term *effective* relates more to simply getting the job done. It can be said that the other customers who were there for food stamps were effective. I am sure that just as Mother did, they received their stamps, although they had to stand in line for most of the day. To the contrary, because of the way Mother was dressed, she avoided the long lines. In other words, her packaging worked efficiently while the other clients' packaging only worked effectively. We might also say, her packaging was like advanced technology—it got the job done at a faster rate of speed. In a nutshell, she got what she wanted, which was food stamps; and she got them using minimal energy and in little time. I see you, Mama.

We all could ask ourselves the question, "How does my packaging work for me?" It does not matter what type packaging it is, whether it is the packaging of a product or service, or how we package our personal selves in the way we speak, write, dress, or post on social media. Consider how your packaging can work for you as technology of efficiency to get what you want with greater speed and less energy expanded.

In closing, always remember that packaging provides an experience for those who witness it and those who handle it. Based on the exterior package, assumptions are made about the quality of the product itself, and responses are made to the product, whether to buy it or leave it on the shelf. Using the example of my mother, she was packaged like a social worker. Because of how she presented herself, the others in the crowd responded by letting her pass in front of them. In essence, they ensured her a position at the front of the line.

What assumptions do people make of you when they see your packaging, or when they see you? Based on how you present yourself, do you look like the consumer, or do you look like the producer? Do you look like a c-suite executive or a line worker? Do you look like the borrower, or do you look like the lender? Do you look like a novice, or do you look like an industry expert? With packaging done right, you are more likely to score big points and yield faster profits like those at the front of the line. **Take a bite! Enjoy the Slice!**

SLICE 5

ARE YOU GENERATING REVENUE OR WEALTH?

I hear several coaches on social media, who say that a greater percentage of what business owners should be doing on a daily basis is generating revenue. Once I was working with an automation tech specialist, who asked me to send over a list of my current projects, more specifically my to-do list. I was happy to send it over, since I generally work by to-do lists.

Upon organizing my weekly tasks, I noticed that what I was doing that week did not seem to generate revenue. Thinking back to what I heard from coaches on social media, I pondered if I was doing something wrong. I even inquired of the tech specialist what she thought of my weekly activities. Being of the mind that the larger percent of your time should be allocated to generating revenue, she replied, "You're having an aha moment, aren't you?"

Rather than respond, I took a closer look at my to-do list. I was honestly starting to become just a little bit concerned, at least enough to evaluate my activities for that week. It was clear that there were hardly any quick money makers on my list. I noticed an interesting pattern, however. While most of my activities did not seem to be revenue generating, they were wealth building instead. At that moment, I had another epiphany: as much as it is important to generate revenue, it is equally important to build and generate wealth. In my case, I was devoting more attention to projects that, over time, would yield huge value for me and my business. It did not take long before I realized that generating revenue often comes from quick money-making tasks. This might be considered the type of activity that helps to ensure that you have a steady income stream from sales. This certainly has its place of importance. That said, I would not tell anybody that generating revenue is not essential. Still, you want to be sure that you are also generating wealth, keeping in mind that these types of activities take longer to yield profit over time.

Think about stocks and mutual funds and other investment vehicles. Financial advisors and financial planners may tell you; this is not something where you are going to see an overnight return. Again, activities that are directly tied to wealth may take longer to complete and most often take longer to reveal gains. Let's consider the following three seeds for the unique perspective they add to our understanding around the role of wealth and revenue in business and in life.

1st Seed: Revenue is the 'heart' that pays expenses.

It does not matter how much revenue you generate; most of what you earn is allocated toward paying for one expense or another, whether the expense recurs every month, such as a utility bill, or an expense paid over a long time, as in a mortgage note.

As a business owner, you incur regular expenses like fuel for your automobile; payroll and related taxes, payments made to your contractors; your cell phone bill, internet, and cable; insurances; office supplies, equipment, technology software, and the list goes on. These have several things in common—all are expenses that are typically paid from revenue, revenue we generate, deposit into our bank accounts, and withdraw at the appropriate time. Even after you paid all your expenses throughout the year, and you are left with your end-of-the-year net profit, what you have remaining is the amount you carry over for next year's cycle of expenses. Again, your revenue has a specific role, and that is to pay your expenses.

If we think of sales as the *heartbeat* of the company, revenue might then be described as the *heart* itself. Just like the heart pumps blood throughout the body, revenue pumps payments to your vendors, contractors, and employees, which are all a part of your company's expenses. It can be said that without sales, there is no sign of life in the company. And without the revenue to pump payments to the vendors, the company is without the necessary technology, supplies, and services to sustain in getting its products and services to its customers.

ALICIA D. RITCHEY, Ed.D.

To clarify this point, let's say you owned a construction company. If month after month, you made no sales, before long, you would have to consider closing the doors of your company. This is what is meant when I refer to your sales as the *heartbeat* of your company. If the heart stops beating, unless the person is resuscitated, soon, the individual will be pronounced dead. The same goes with sales (the company's heartbeat). Without sales, the company is soon likely to close its business doors.

We can use the same example of the construction company to demonstrate how revenue can be termed the *heart* of the company. Let's say the owner has a project of installing sidewalks in a neighborhood. Midway the project, the owner runs out of funds, and is no longer able to finish paying the contractor to pour the concrete. Having no revenue to pay the contractor for the concrete, how will the owner complete the sidewalk project? That is why I referred to the revenue as the heart of the company. As mentioned, the *heart* is responsible for pumping blood throughout the body; otherwise, the individual would be threatening a heart attack, a stroke, and even loss of limbs due to lack of blood flow. Relative to the owner in our example, the company's revenue (the heart) has the responsibility of pumping payment of funds (blood) to the contractors, other vendors, and employees. Without the circulation of funds to the vendors, the health of the company is comprised, where the limbs of the company, namely contractors, other vendors, and employees would expectedly fall off.

2nd Seed: Wealth is the 'brain' that pays legacy.

Remember, unlike revenue, which pays bills and expenses, wealth pays legacy. I should first explain how I define wealth. Many people view wealth simply as an outcome or product of an abundance of goods or money. In the context of which I am speaking, fundamentally, wealth can be described as a cycle of content, process, and product. At the point of content, wealth is a growth mindset of abundance. What flows from a wealth or growth mindset is a well-designed process, namely strategy that includes systems and procedures to manage resources, to produce high-quality products and services, and to generate a steady flow of revenue through sales. In this cycle, the outcome or product of wealth is a lived reality of perpetual prosperity and ever-ascending profitability, where the possibility of lack or depletion does not exist.

Think of wealth as the *brain* or control center of your company. Using the brain as a metaphor to describe wealth, then we can better understand how wealth should function within our business, and even our everyday lives. To draw the comparison between wealth and the brain, I share three important research findings about the brain, conclusions that apply to wealth and its relationship to your overall business operation.

Point 1: Most scientists agree that the brain establishes order for the human body in that it controls and regulates all bodily functions, including our thought, memory, emotion, touch, motor skills, vision, breathing, temperature, and hunger. Like the brain, wealth can be viewed as the control center for your business. If properly set up, then wealth—the business *brain*—serves as a guide to regulate every decision made by the business owner. Acting In the role of the brain, in a nutshell, wealth sets the intention of the business towards generational success and provides the necessary strategy to ensure growth, sustainability, and profitability.

Point 2: Known as the seat of intelligence, the brain sends messages through the nerves to the rest of the body. Without the brain sending those messages, the body cannot properly perform its various functions. In the case of business, wealth is the seat of expansion, exponential multiplication, and sustainability. Wealth sends messages of efficiency, productivity, profitability to every aspect of the business, whether sales and marketing, management and administration, or product development and service delivery. Without being directed by wealth, acting as the business *brain*, the various parts of the business operation, instead of working as a cohesive unit, are not able to properly function and sustain toward meeting its goal and completing its mission.

Point 3: The brain detects and reads external stimuli. As part of the brain, the amygdala steadily monitors our environment to gauge for our safety level and reads the environment for indicators of impending danger. Essentially, this portion of the brain has the primary goal of ensuring our safety and defending us against harm. Similarly, wealth ensures that the company has built in safeguards for reducing and overcoming risks. Whether the risks are political, environmental, supply-based, economic, competitive, legal, or otherwise, like the brain, wealth is able to read these external conditions to determine when to pivot and make adjustments within the operation.

Ironically, people tend to start businesses to generate revenue to meet their immediate needs but fail to see the important role wealth plays in directing revenue acquisition; hence revenue, even when easily obtained, is likely to run out. In essence, the business may have a *heart* but may lack a *brain,* in which case, the heart may be steadily pumping with no brain activity, working everyday merely to generate revenue, with no wealth in sight and no legacy in mind.

3rd Seed: Legacy is not only for those who come after you; legacy is also for you.

Legacy is most often thought of as money or property that one leaves for another in a will. It is intended that with legacy, or what is left behind, the quality of someone's life is improved. It is not often, however, that people include themselves in their own legacy. If we were to consider legacy as "impact or consequence, what remains and is set aside from our past work," then we would adjust how we define legacy to include ourselves, not just others. Seen in this light, what we have saved in our retirement then is not just what we leave behind for others. Instead, part of our legacy is what we can reap and enjoy when we leave behind our career or our business.

Keep in mind, whether you retire from a 9 to 5 career, or whether you decide you no longer want to continue your business endeavors, your to-do list should not only focus on generating revenue for today; but must include activities that will sustain you both now and in your legacy years. Otherwise, you run the risk of being over-worked like a stressed heart, generating revenue for today without storing up treasure for tomorrow, with no legacy to leave behind for others nor for your own future.

In conclusion, ask yourself, "If what I'm doing isn't generating money for today, does it generate wealth for my tomorrow?" And if, in fact, what you are doing will help position you for a better tomorrow, you may be doing what is more important. Yes. These activities may take longer time, but that's okay. Because again, the work you do should not be for the purpose of only generating revenue. You should also be generating wealth. And if you're going to generate wealth, it means that a portion of your time is going to be allocated to that activity, as well.

Remember, a major objective of wealth is ascending profitability. In a traditional sense, a true mark of wealth is its ability to create a legacy of sustainability, so that wealth is prolonged over generations. We can reference back to our description of wealth as the business *brain*, where wealth drives every decision made by the business owner. This means that the business owner does not make arbitrary decisions about the business operation. Instead, the owner submits to the principle of wealth in terms of how the business should operate. Inspired by a wealth mindset, the owner ensures that everything in the operation supports its intention toward legacy. Therefore, a portion of the revenue is put into wealth building vehicle, so that wealth and revenue engage in an ebb and flow relationship, whereby wealth generates more revenue, and revenue helps to generate more wealth. Remember, revenue is purposed to be spent, and is, therefore, temporal. Wealth is purposed to be sustained, and is, therefore, perpetual. **Take a bite! Enjoy the Slice!**

SLICE 6

PRODUCTS OR SERVICES: WHERE DOES THE MONEY RESIDE?

I once heard a presentation by Robert Kiyosaki where he made a case for why product-based businesses are more likely to generate more wealth than service-based businesses. When you think about it, he makes sense. He argues that a well-designed business has built-in assets, meaning whether you are providing a service or not, your company is able to generate wealth. The question you ask yourself is: "If your company were to pause the service that it provides, would you still generate revenue?" If you answered "No," then you may want to consider how you can build assets into your company. Your assets will allow you to generate revenue and build wealth in your sleep without you lifting a finger.

If you own a tax preparation company, for example, and you stop providing the service of preparing taxes, how would your company generate revenue? If your company isn't likely to generate revenue because you're not providing service, then Robert Kiyosaki would call that a poor company. But a rich company is one that has assets, whether these are products you currently sell or something you own of value which can be sold (i.e., books, apparel, real estate, courses, etc.). Again, rich companies or wealthy companies have assets built into them.

I mentioned a book among the list of assets that you can own. You may be thinking, "I do not have a story to tell." Of course, you do! And that story could be about your experience as a first, second, or 20-year entrepreneur. In fact, every day that you are providing the service, you can chronicle your experience and package it into a book. Now you have not only a service, but also an asset. If you develop a methodology and list step by step how to complete a task, those steps can be converted into a curriculum, a manual or guide that has value as an asset. Imagine how you can also license that curriculum to generate more wealth. So, it is not just the product itself, but when you license the use of the product to someone else, the product or asset has even greater wealth building potential. Other assets include your intellectual property, such as registered trademarks of your company (logos, taglines, etc.) These have worth and add value to your company and its brand. You may have heard about people developing brands only to have someone else come along and steal them. While you may be sleeping on your assets, other people understand that whatever you put time and energy into developing, it has value. Now, let's see what we can harvest from our three seeds.

1st Seed: Experiences are assets too.

One of the beauties of experiences is that no two people share the exact same life journey. Therefore, we each have our own experiences, not to mention our unique retelling, interpretations, and take-aways from our experiences. If you were to speak with two siblings, born and reared by the same parents, the narratives of their lives, in terms of how they perceive their experiences would be vastly different. Some of this is due to birth order, changes in parental dynamics, socioeconomic status, lived and historical encounters, personal values, etc.

    As an example, I am born as the seventh child in a family of nine siblings, all sharing the same parents. My three older siblings were born during the early years of my parents' marriage when my parents were young and still trying to navigate their way through life, especially while transitioning from small town to big city. During that time, resources were not as plentiful, and extended family members of grandparents, aunts, and uncles also played a vital role in helping with our family survival. By the time the latter siblings reached our teenage years, my parents were more settled and financially secure. My father's painting business was booming; and my mother had left her profession as a cosmetologist to pursue higher education and to become a university administrator.

    If you ask my siblings and me what it was like being raised by our parents, we would each have different stories, based on our individual experiences. Though unique in details, you can expect valuable lessons, life strategies, meaningful advice, inspiration, and humor from all our stories. One of my siblings packages her life experiences into products of spoken word and poetry books, sharing them with audiences across the globe. Another of my siblings is a storyteller. She packages and shares her experiences into folktales and inspirational genre.

Like my siblings and I, you also have experiences, perhaps an active part of your memory that you share at family gatherings. Or perhaps, the memory of those experiences is lying dormant in the deep recesses of your mind, disregarded and forgotten. Whatever you choose to do with them, your life experiences have value. Package them into products, convert them into assets, and get them sold in the marketplace. To do otherwise would be an utter waste of wealth.

2nd Seed: Service-based businesses rely on product-based businesses to thrive.

A major reason product-based businesses are so valuable is because service-based businesses rely on them to thrive. If you have a service-based business, perhaps you have never considered the myriad of products you use to meet consumer demands. For example, a barber, who builds a hair-cutting business, goes to a product-based business to buy the clippers.

Further to this point, consider the various tasks involved in the fulfillment of a single contract. Think about it. Just to communicate with your client, you need a device, whether a cellphone, land line phone, or computer. To send a proposal, contract, or invoice, you use a smart phone or computer, and accounting software. What if you need to store your data? Another product you might use is a cloud-based platform. If you use hard copies, you will typically print the paper- work, which means you need paper and ink products; and possibly a file cabinet to store your file folders. Imagine all the other products you use to manage this process.

What about when you deliver the service? Let's say you are an educational trainer, and you were awarded a contract that required you to do a live training. Now you might need other products, including a laptop, a mouse, a projector, and a screen. Wherever you are in meeting your obligations (preparation, delivery, assessment, and contract closure), there is a long list of products you will need. It is conceivable that before the fulfillment period closes, you may have used ten to twenty products.

We don't often think of product-based businesses using service-based businesses to the same degree. We can imagine, however, owners of product-based businesses are in expectation that service-based business owners are en route, searching for a line of products today and more products tomorrow. If this is the case, product-based business owners stand a chance to generate more revenue and subsequently more wealth, because of the likelihood that someone is soon coming to buy from their product lines.

3rd Seed: There is a season of strength and a season of wisdom.

We may not realize how much of our lives operate within the parameters of seasons. Like clockwork, the seasons change, and we take heed to govern ourselves accordingly. For example, by seasons, we know what outdoor activities we should be doing at a certain time of year, how we should dress, what foods we should eat, etc. Overall, how we live our lives depends heavily on the season we are in.

Seasons represent change, which is a natural part of our everyday existence. For those who live to see retirement age, there are obvious

ALICIA D. RITCHEY, Ed.D.

changes we start to notice, including interests, daily activities, and working schedules. This change tells us that the person has entered a new season of life. As familiar as we may be with seasons, sometimes the transition from one season to another could suggest that one is approaching the end of life. Unlike the seasons of nature, the change from younger to older happens on a continuum instead of a rotation. Life as a continuum, toward an ending point, can sometimes feel uncomfortable to process. If you ever had the pleasure of spending time with elderly persons, you know that one of their greatest fears is that one day, they will no longer be relevant in the spaces they once occupied, or they will no longer have worth, and may soon be forgotten. Sometimes, what may contribute to their fear is the steady decline in their strength, mobility, and perhaps memory. While changing seasons are imminent, it helps when people know that their lives can have perpetual value and that they will be remembered long after they are gone.

I view our business life as having two primary seasons—a season of strength and a season of wisdom. I refer to those years of heavy lifting as the season of strength. The more relaxed laid-back years, I refer to as the season of wisdom. The truth is that on the continuum of life, the seasons of strength and wisdom are timed just right. After all, it was never intended that we spend our older years in business doing the same sometimes-arduous work we did when we were younger, in our season of strength.

We might say that when we are most involved in the development of products and services for our business, we are demonstrating strength. On the other hand, the season where you focus more on passing down knowledge around principles, strategies, and best practices, this may be called the season of wisdom. In reality, there may come a time in your business where you may not be able to demonstrate strength, or you may choose not to continue providing a particular service. Should this happen, you don't have to fear that you will soon be forgotten. You can maintain relevance in the marketplace through your products. Your assets, whether tangible products or intellectual properties, are all monuments of wisdom that preserve the memory of your impact on your industry, and on your contribution to the collective body of work within a particular discipline. Additionally, so long as you have a presence in the marketplace, you can continue generating revenue and wealth for you and your legacy. Remember a well-designed business has built-in assets. When you have preserved your wisdom in product form, that wisdom will have perpetual value.

In summary, while your business may be service-based, it helps to have assets that include products which can be packaged and sold. In this way, the sustainability of your company does not rely solely on the physical presence of you and your team for said service; where, in your absence, you miss the opportunity to generate revenue for your company. On the other hand, with products as assets, your company can generate revenue while you are asleep.

Assets can vary in a range of forms. Some common assets include real estate, trademarks, patents, and copyrighted material. One type of asset often overlooked by business owners is books. Your experiences have monetary value. Capture the stories of your life in book form. Share the lessons learned from your experiences. Now, your life journey becomes a revenue generating asset.

So where does the money reside? I would argue that the money resides both in product and service-based businesses. However, the greatest opportunity to generate revenue is wherever you can replicate productivity in mass. This is more likely to be in product form. ***Take a bite! Enjoy the Slice!***

SLICE 7

RETURN OF THE REVOLUTION.

Gil Scott-Heron was an American poet from the seventies and eighties, who became widely known for his spoken-word performances. One of his pieces described social change as a *revolution*, whose impact would be a turning point in our society. I think most of us will agree that during the Covid-19 Pandemic, our global society has experienced a *revolution*. By making a distinction between *evolution* and *revolution*, I intend to help clarify where I am going with this Slice.

When we think of evolution, we think of growth and progress, where things are moving forward in the same direction. Revolution, on the other hand, suggests a change in direction, a disruption, if you like. I am not saying that a revolution is necessarily a turn away from progress, or a movement in backward motion. Instead, *revolution* might be viewed as a shift from the status quo, a reexamination and review of how we operate, sometimes making as much as a 180 degrees turn. Within our present-day society, a major shift is certainly visible, and beyond a doubt, we are in the eye of a revolution. Times are changing, and business owners are feeling the need to pivot, especially with changes in people's priorities when it comes to goods and services, and how they access these goods and services.

We, as business owners, have some decisions to make as we move through the changing tides brought on by the revolution. We must decide if we are going to pack our bags and go home, or if we are going to stay on course. If we decide to endure the race, we must decide what adjustments are necessary for us to have relevance and influence in the marketplace. Let us examine the seeds inside this Slice. Perhaps we can find something to help us to remain focused in this present-day revolution.

1st Seed: The revolution did not seek our permission to be, but it provides new opportunities.

As mentioned, the Pandemic unquestionably ushered in a revolution that many did not foresee. Just like that, change occurred, and without notice too. Therefore, when we build our businesses, and our lives in general, we must consider that change is imminent, and that it may sometimes occur at the most unexpected times. We must be flexible enough as entrepreneurs that we are not caught so far off guard that we are ultimately forced to close our businesses due to changes brought on by change. Furthermore, we must be fluid enough that the tentacles of our businesses have broad reach across demographics, industries, and service types. As a case in point, we can use again the example of a seamstress, who may have started a business designing original pieces or redesigning existing pieces for celebrities. Given the revolution of changes brought on by the Pandemic, we saw a shift in demands, which resulted in an increasing need for masks and other related products and services. Should the seamstress become so etched in providing a single service that she is not able to take advantage of the opportunities that emerged in the revolution? If she is flexible and poised for immediate pivot, when governments and corporations made it mandatory for their employees to wear masks, this could have been a major advancement for the seamstress, and even Mom and Pop businesses. This shows us that the revolution, though unpredictable in its timing and nature, poses challenges and new opportunities.

2nd Seed: Revolutions shift what's important in our society.

In today's revolution, we must think about what is important in this present hour. With this concern, we are seeing that now, more than before, people are thinking about matters such as cyber security, advanced technology, mental health, fitness, financial literacy, credit building, business development, sanitation, etc. Therefore, as we consider launching and scaling our businesses, we may have to make some adjustments in terms of the solutions we can provide, considering what is important to people right now.

Again, we must keep in mind that while businesses generate profits for business owners, how much business owners profit from their businesses depends on the problems that they are able to solve, and the needs that are filled by the products and services they provide. So, as the needs of society shift, proprietors must be malleable enough to bend our products and services to meet the current needs. Remember the revolution does not always come with warning, therefore, from the outset, we must build our businesses as flexible entities with a wide range of motion, in terms of our target audiences and their demographics, our service offerings, and how we get our products to our prospective clientele. If we're going to stay in the race, we cannot narrowly design our business models. And, even when we create products, we must think about how our specific products can have multidisciplinary value across diverse demographics.

3rd Seed: The revolution will be up close and personal, not just televised.

When Gil Scott-Heron wrote his piece on the revolution, he described how the revolution would make a live appearance, and not appear through media such as television, radio, or print. If we draw from Scott-Heron's poem and compare it with what business owners currently face, we see that the present-day revolution demands that we come from behind the glass to get in the faces of our prospective clients. By face-to-face, I do not mean literally by person-to-person. I mean building a sense of community with your clientele. This requires that we show up on social media, in their emails, and via phone calls and texts. Our clients must know that we are in the room. Competition is fiercer than it has ever been. Joining this competition doesn't mean that you have to say to your competitor, "I want your client." You must, however, let your own clients know that you are present, available, and ready to serve.

We must show up in such a way that to our consumer, it

does not feel like we are simply appearing on the other side of the television or computer screen, so to speak, or as if we are reading a monologue taken from a script. The consumer must feel like they are having a shared experience with us, and that they are engaging with us in live authentic conversations that connect to the heart and soul of the people; especially those with whom we are building a transactional relationship.

The present-day revolution, live on the scene, requires that we show up ready with raised innovation, visibility, and accessibility. As I mentioned earlier, the competition is fierce! People are hungry and some are greedy. In the same way that the revolution returned without our permission, we need to show up unapologetically energetic in our convictions. If not, we could get pushed out and off the playing field, without our permission.

In summary, the revolution has returned. It came without asking our permission. With the shift comes challenges that we must overcome as business owners. Along with the challenges, however, comes new opportunities that can catapult us to the next stage of growth in operations, productivity, and profitability. Seeing that the revolution returned at a time that we perhaps did not even expect, my advice is that we design our businesses as flexible multi-faceted entities, with reach across various demographics, areas of service, and industry sectors. Finally, we must be determined to get in the faces of our clientele, to show up live and in living color, in terms of the experiences we provide, the relationships we build, and the easy access to the goods we offer, bringing our business brands to their front door and into their living room. **Take a bite! Enjoy the Slice!**

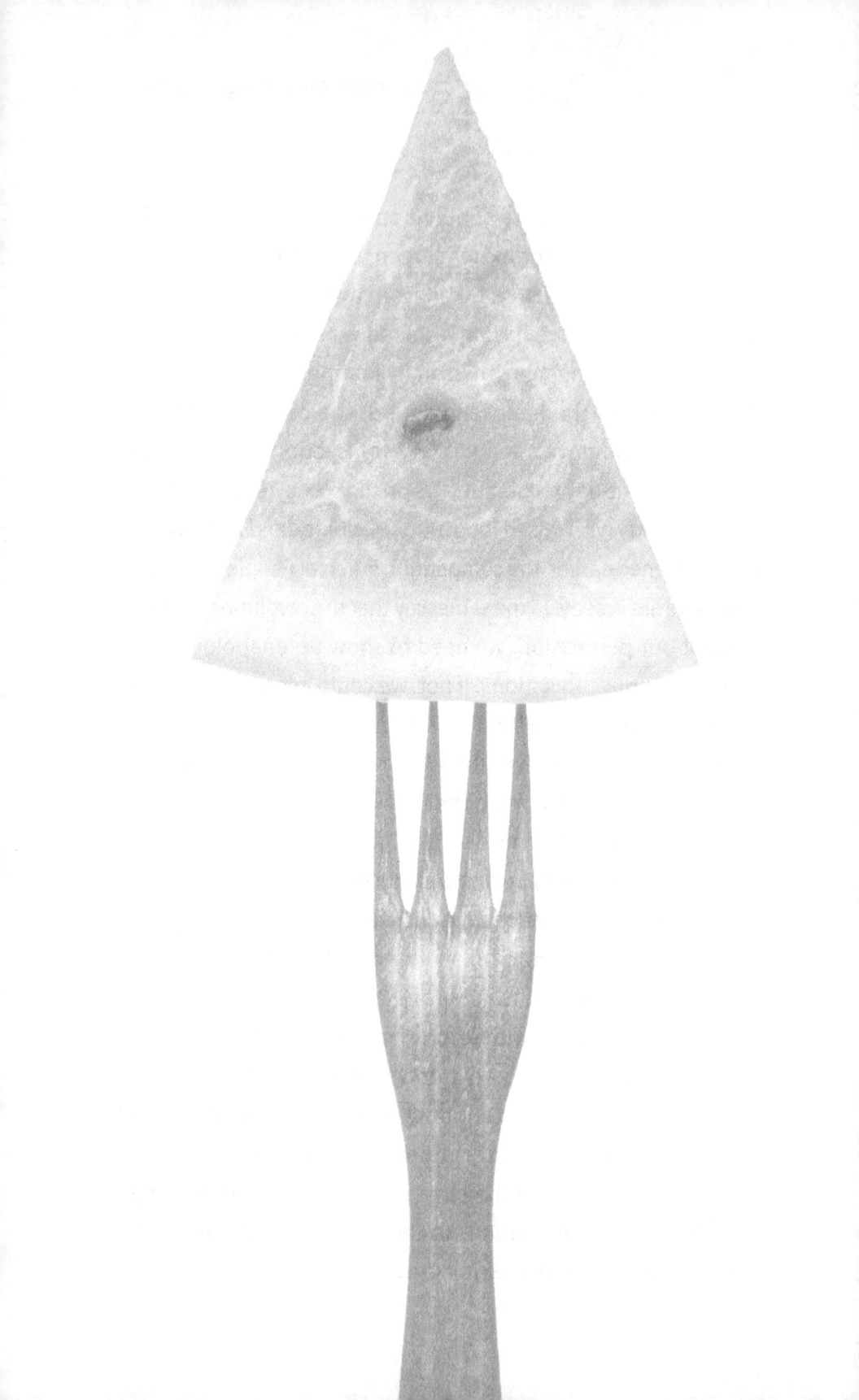

SLICE 8

SHHH…
THE TERMITES ARE SPEAKING.

The topic of this Slice relates to a lesson that I learned after relocating from big city Miami, Florida to live with my parents in rural small-town Cordele, Georgia. At the back of our house in Cordele was a screened-in porch. So that I would have a place to conduct business, my parents enclosed the screened-in area, which I used as my home office. After a few years in the space, I started noticing mounds of dirt on the walls. I had never seen anything like that before. I was friends with a local contractor, and I asked him, "What is the cause of the dirt on the walls?" He told me not to worry about it, and that this was typical in South Georgia. While this occurrence seemed odd, I simply brushed the walls to remove the dirt and continued as usual.

At this time, my parents had traveled back to Florida, and so I relied on the advice of the contractor. Another instance, I noticed that the mounds of dirt had returned. In fact, every so often, I would see the dirt on the wall, and since I had already been told that this was commonplace for Southwest Georgia, I did my usual routine—sweeping the walls, removing the dirt, dumping the dirt into the trash, though never feeling settled that this was normal.

This went on for some time, until one day, I went into the office, and without turning on the light, I noticed something different about one of the pictures on the office wall. There was a strange darkness about the picture. I switched on the lights to see that there were termites inside the glass frame. I took down the picture and found that there were gaping holes in the wall. The termites had come out of the ground, and from behind the aluminum siding. They ate through the exterior wood and the drywall. They also ate through the cardboard paper on the back of the frame to reach the front of the picture inside the frame.

I started to think about those mounds of dirt that I had previously seen on the walls. Little did I know that the dirt mounds were evidence of a major problem. What the contractor described as normal turned out to be an army of termites that were slowly but surely bringing destruction to the entire back of the house. When I called the termite company, the gentlemen showed me how soft the walls had become. He went around the room, and with just two of his fingers, he pressed several areas of the walls, including the door frames and the frames around the windows. The termites caused so much damage, we had to rebuild the entire office.

I recall being thoroughly disturbed when I saw how many termites were inside the picture frame. In fact, I had to sit down and take a moment to gather myself. While sitting, I reflected on the full experience, from the mounds of dirt all the way to the live termites swirling behind the glass of the picture frame. In my stillness, I had a light bulb moment: you can learn a lot from termites. I thought of how people often say, "This happened suddenly," or "suddenly this appeared." Based on my experience with the termites, my notion of the term 'suddenly' completely shifted. In the following seeds, we examine what the termites have to teach us about 'suddenly' and its gradual unveiling.

1st Seed: 'Suddenly' is evidence that something was already taking place.

People often use the term 'suddenly' to speak of something appearing from out of nowhere. However, using the example of the termites, *suddenly* is more aptly defined as the final manifestation of what has been in process over time. Just because you or I did not see it coming does not mean that something has not already been transpiring. In other words, *suddenly* comes with preparation and prior activity, whether you see the activity or not. Take the lesson from the termites.

Prior to visibly seeing the termites, the termites had already been active—they came from out of the ground and behind the aluminum siding to eat through the exterior wood, the drywall, and the cardboard paper on the back of the picture frame, to reach the front of picture inside the glass. Taking this example, we might say that, in this instance, it was my sudden recognition of the termites' activity that occurred in the moment. However, the point of my recognition was not the point at which the termites became active. The progression of the termites' activity transpired without my knowing, and because I was not aware of the presence of the termites, I could not acknowledge what was occurring. Hmmmmm. We can't acknowledge that which we have no awareness.

So where was the real *suddenly*? We might say that what 'suddenly' took place was my recognition of the termites, and not their presence and activity. In other words, the termites were alive, present, and active; suddenly, I took note of their activity. So, *suddenly* is not only the final manifestation of what those termites had been doing all that time; suddenly is also the moment at which I became aware of what had been happening all along.

2nd Seed: 'Suddenly' happens by design or by default depending on how you use your time.

The termites wreaked havoc, but that did not occur in a single moment. The destruction they caused was done over a period of time. Again, what I saw in the moment was the manifestation of their extended prolonged activity. The termites used their time to design and successfully execute the destruction of an entire room. *Design* then is the strategic and intentional use of time and other resources to outline and create your desired outcome. We can say, on the other hand, that *default* is the outcome you must live with and settle for because of your negligible use of time and other resources. This applies to anyone, in any situation.

Think about the outcome or 'suddenly' that you want. Given what you say you want, will this happen by *design* because you not only planned; you were also strategic and intentional about how you used time to create your desired outcome? Or is your 'suddenly' going to be by *default* because you were negligent with your use of time? Remember, if it is by *design*, it is because you will use time and other resources to be strategic and intentional about creating that outcome. If it happens by *default*, you will have to live with the outcome because you perhaps used your time frivolously. Whether by *design* or by *default*, time is a common denominator of the outcome. This means that neither outcome happens overnight. However, *design* and *default* are different in that those who choose the option of *design*, couple their time with strategy, intention, and the execution of a well-thought-out plan. As I witnessed with the termites, the same can be said regarding our businesses and our personal lives.

3rd Seed: Heartbreak is the result of a major opportunity for which you did not use time to prepare.

How often do you hear someone tell of waiting for a big break? Does waiting require that we sit idly, doing nothing? Of course not. Imagine that the major opportunity you have long awaited comes knocking on your door. It comes, however, at a time when you are not prepared to receive it. At that moment, you will likely wish for more time to prepare. In an instance such as this, you can end up feeling heartbroken, not because the opportunity never came, but because you were not ready to receive it. The lack of preparation is likely related to how you managed time. Now, what could have been your big break, the moment you've long awaited, has become the moment you regret.

If there is any lesson to take from this, it is about the value of time in shaping the future. With time in our hands, we have an incredible opportunity to shape our next moment. Moment by moment, we are stitching together pieces of our desired outcome, or by default, you may be stitching together an outcome that you regret. Again, the time of the present moment is one to prepare for the next. This could mean the next client, the next job opportunity, the next major purchase of real estate property. It could even mean the next pandemic. Again, how are you using your time?

Despite what may be said of the recent Pandemic, with the social economic recess, many of us were afforded the luxury of more time. With work-from-home options, we saw closures of schools, government buildings, restaurants, entertainment centers, you name it. For many business owners, there was more time to better design their businesses, create new products and services, build systems, and learn new technology through free on-line programs.

Some took advantage of this season while others, once restrictions were lifted and quarantines dialed back, realized that they had not used that time to their advantage. Time had passed, windows of opportunities slammed shut, and some did not prepare for a rebound of client leads, new business opportunities, funding, and other aspects of business growth.

Many of those business owners who did not take advantage of the opportunities that presented themselves during the Pandemic can attest to the heartbreaks of when opportunity meets unpreparedness. Thankfully, we can ensure a different narrative for ourselves depending on our prior use of time. When our 'suddenly' appears, whether it manifests as an influx of new clients, a boost in business funding, and bookings for major speaking engagements, not only are we ready for it, but we also designed for it.

In summary, *design* is the strategic intentional use of time and other resources to create a desired outcome or to create the *suddenly* you want. *Default*, on the other hand, is the outcome that you must live with or settle for because of your own poor management. What is the outcome you want for your business? Use the time you are given to prepare for it, and design your *suddenly*. Remember *suddenly*, 'out of nowhere,' is more a myth than a reality. There is always some activity that precedes *suddenly.* And you can be strategic and intentional to create the *suddenly* that you want. Finally, heartbreak is the result of a major opportunity that turned into a major catastrophe, simply because of the lack of preparation. Be sure that your *suddenly* is by design and not by default. **Take a bite! Enjoy your Slice!**

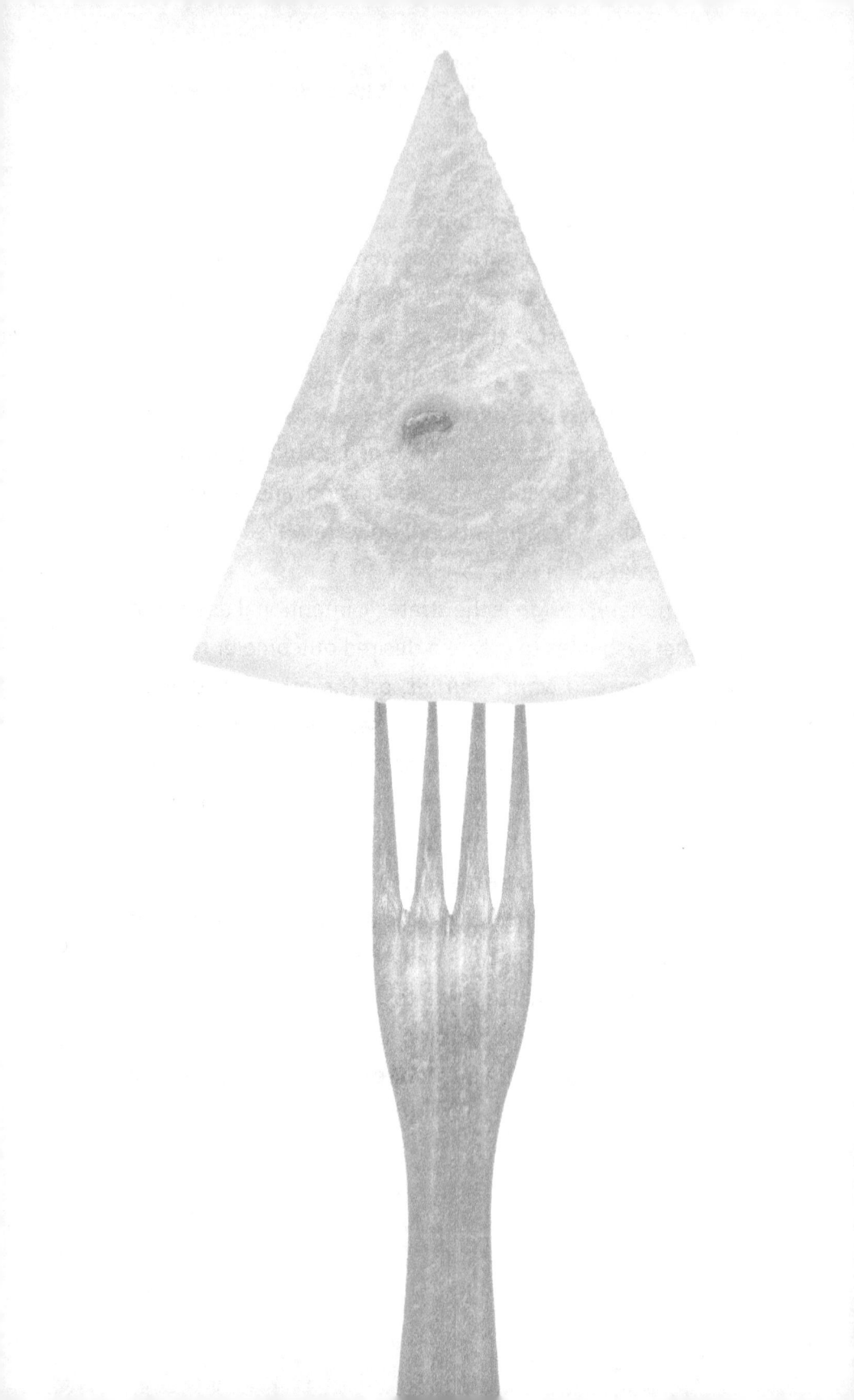

SLICE 9

PITCHING TO THE RIGHT CLIENT.

The topic of this Slice comes from an experience I had when I was about 19 years old. One day, I was riding the local transit en route to class at Miami Dade College. While on the bus, I saw an older male cousin who beckoned me to sit near him at the rear of the bus. I followed his lead and went to a seat next to where he was sitting. Across from us sat a woman who seemed interested in our conversation. Quite honestly, I could not really blame the woman seeing that my cousin was being obnoxious—speaking loudly enough such that everyone on the bus could probably hear what he was saying to me.

From time to time, the people on the bus looked at us. However, the woman sitting across from us stared incessantly at my cousin and me as we continued speaking. After a while, my cousin became irritated by her long stares. He finally responded in an embarrassingly very dramatic and matter-of-fact tone. He looked directly at the woman, though still speaking to me, he said, "Cousin, somebody is listening, but I want you to hear it."

ALICIA D. RITCHEY, Ed.D.

In other words, "I'm talking to you, Alicia, but she's all up in our business." While she briefly looked away, it wasn't long before she turned again to stare in our direction, clearly wanting to hear what we had to say.

My cousin's words stayed with me for a long time, and so did the idea that he would speak so loudly, as if to engage others, including the staring woman, but then to react harshly to the woman's interest in what he was saying. What could he possibly have expected? While the incident with my cousin happened nearly forty years ago, it came to mind again, most recently when my parents, at their home in Miami, received a visit from a family friend, a highly skilled and well-sought-after craftsman. During his visit, he shared with us an incident he had with one of his wealthy clients, who asked him to bid on a residential project she needed to complete. The woman knew the value of our friend's work and had used him several times for previous projects. After evaluating the project, he estimated that it would only take a couple of hours to complete. He offered a bid of $800, and a competitor offered a $4,000 bid for the same job. After the client considered the two bids, she opted to use the contractor with the $4,000 bid. Taken aback by the client's choice of the higher bid, our friend asked her why she did not select him to do the work. She replied, "Listen, I don't need you to feel sorry for me when it comes to placing a bid. I have money. I know the quality of your work, but if you do not know the value of your work, I don't need you working for me."

Obviously, he learned the lesson quickly. Shortly thereafter, her friend called him to bid on another project. This time, for a job that would take one hour to complete, he gave a bid of nearly four times the amount of the bid he offered the previous client. As he shared the story, he showed us the deposit check that the second client had given him to start the job.

While we were drawn into his recount of the entire experience, we were most amazed by the response of the first client, who told him, "I know the quality of your work, but if you do not know the value of your work, I don't need you working for me." That statement resonated with me as a business owner. I could see three important elements of sales that should accompany every pitch: quality, confidence, and boldness. The contractor must offer a quality product or service. The contractor must be confident regarding the value of the product or service and its positive impact on the client. Then the contractor must be bold enough to make the ask!

As our friend was sharing the story, I thought about the magazines that I publish every quarter. I considered how much time goes into creating each issue, from the point of selecting what personalities to feature, to the photo shoots in preparation of the feature stories, from the layout and design, to editing, to printing, to prepping the envelopes for shipping, and the list goes on. Besides the magazines, I reflected on the other products and services that my business offers, and what it takes to develop, launch, and ensure that these goods reach the masses.

I compared the time it takes me to produce and deliver my products and services to the time it would take our friend to do the jobs requested by his clients, a single hour in one instance and two hours in another instance. In just the brief moments of being in conversation with our family friend, his experience prompted me to evaluate my prices—the price of each edition of the magazine and the suite of other products and services I offer. That was when I realized that my prices were far too low. However, all was not lost. I discovered the missing link in my sales pitch. I have a quality product and service. I am confident in the transformative value of what I offer. What I lacked was the boldness to make the ask. Why? Partly because I was pitching to the wrong client. Repeatedly, I replayed in my head the words of our friend's client, "I know the quality of your work, but if you do not know the value of your work, I don't need you working for me." Could it be that the right client is one who knows the quality of my work and expects that I know the value of my work, and then charge accordingly?

I also remembered my cousin who said, "Somebody listening, but I want you to hear it." Perhaps, the person we want to hear is not the person who is listening. As embarrassing as it was to hear my cousin speak to the woman on the bus in the manner he did, within the context of business, his words are applicable to sales and marketing, and identifying your ideal client. The following seeds address these aspects of business.

1st Seed: Who is listening is also who is interested.

When you identify those who are listening, you also know who is interested. Going back to the incident on the bus with my cousin, the woman was staring and listening because she was interested in what we were saying. If my cousin and I were salespersons, she would be what we would call low-hanging fruit. We would not have to work hard to make a pitch because we already had her attention. The same goes for your business sales. When you already have a group that's interested in what you are saying and selling, pitching becomes that much easier.

There is an entire discipline of market research, where people study the demographics of consumers who are interested in their products and services. Notice, if you click on a particular social media ad, you start to see other products and services that are similar. Your initial click is a sign of interest. Based on your demographics and your browsing history, advertisers can predict whether you will pause to listen or watch, and how likely you are to click the 'buy now' button.

Think about your own business and ask yourself, who's listening. You may be talking to someone, but is the person to whom you are directing your message the same person who is showing interest? Are they buying your products? Using the example of my cousin and me on the bus, he was talking to me, but other people were listening. Although he felt that the woman was being nosey, she was, in fact, buying into our conversation. Similarly, as it relates to your products and services, the person whose attention you have is the person who will listen to your pitch, and is more likely to buy what you are selling.

2nd Seed: Once you identify the listeners, package the product, and take it to that group.

In the instance of the magazine, I assumed that because the feature stories were centered around Black life that the only persons interested would be Black folks since these were their daily life experiences. Perhaps the person having the experience is not the person who is interested in reading about the experience. What about the sea of others, who don't live the Black experience, but can still relate to the stories through a different lens, besides race? What if the fact that others have not experienced black life is the very reason for their interest? By only selling to the Blacks in my community, I was missing out on opportunities found in other markets. I was also restricting my sales to the affordability of those in my target population, who, interestingly, were not my largest consumer base, although the stories were about people they know.

Instead of directing my sales pitch solely to the local communities of those being featured in the magazines, how would my sales perform if I were to get the publication on the shelves at Walmart, in Walgreens, in CVS, in Barnes and Nobles, in Publix, in Whole Foods, and in Target? If these retailers are my potential clients, then I may need to have to package the magazines differently. Packaging to attract these clients may require an ISBN number on the back cover and certain disclaimers inside the publication. These clients may also require that my product meets a list of specifications that are not necessary when selling to an individual or local readership.

In a previous Slice, we spoke of packaging. In this instance, when I speak of packaging, not only am I referring to the product, but I am also speaking of the legitimacy of your company to conduct business at a high level. For example, to get your products on the shelves at mainstream stores, your company may have to carry certain licenses or certifications and maintain certain insurances limits. You may have to show ownership of intellectual properties to prove that you have the right to use certain marks and phrases. Additionally, you may be required to disclose if the content is copyrighted under someone else's name.

So, here, when we think of packaging, think of a product or service inside a box. The company would be the box that contains the product or service. Both the box and what is inside would need to be presented (or packaged) in a way that meets the requirements of the existing and potential client, those who are "listening." If this is the case, there's no need to miss the sale. Simply, package the product or service according to the client's specifications, so that you can meet the listeners where they are, whether they are in mainstream retail stores, on Wall Street, in government buildings, in public education systems, or in the corporate private sector.

3rd Seed: Do not confuse your paying clientele with your beneficiary.

Many times, people start businesses with the intention to serve a particular clientele. Further along, they may find that the population targeted by the business owner is not always the ones taking interest in the owner's products and services. The owners can still serve both groups, where one may be a client and the other a beneficiary. A beneficiary could be the person that you want to reap benefits from your business, those to whom you direct your philanthropic efforts. In the words of my cousin, the beneficiary may be the person "you want to hear."

One might say, "I have a heart for women, and that's who I want to serve." However, the buying demographic may solely be men. Should this happen, it would make sense to sell your products and services to those who are drawn to your brand message, those interested in buying—those who are listening. Make them your target since they are likely to become your paying clientele.

Your clients and beneficiaries are related in that they both experience the best of what you have to offer. Your clients reap from your products and services while your beneficiaries reap from your philanthropy. It is the revenue you earn from paying clients that helps you serve your beneficiaries, perhaps through charitable donations or even your involvement with programs centered around teaching them life skills. So, you can service both groups, but you need to understand who they are as it relates to your business. Is this the beneficiary, or is this your client? Unlike the clients—those who "are listening," the beneficiaries—those you "want to hear," are not likely going to be the ones paying for your products and services. Get the revenue from your "listeners," and allocate a portion of that revenue to those you want to help attain a better quality of life.

In summary, understand that the people who are listening and those you want to hear, may be two different groups. The people that you want to hear your message are not necessarily the people who are interested and willing to buy. Keep in mind that when you pitch to the right client, you can make those wild unthinkable asks, increasing your chances of making high volume sales, and reaping bountiful profits. ***Take a bite! Enjoy the Slice!***

SLICE 10

NO GOLFING INSIDE THE WAREHOUSE.

I recall a time around the year 2000 when I was taking tennis lessons. In the class was a wealthy couple: Kenny and Charlene. After each lesson, they would always say, "Alicia, come and join us for lunch." I would always say, "No, because I have to get back to the office." Time after time, I missed the opportunity to enjoy lunch and build a wonderful relationship away from the tennis court. At that time, I was co-owner of a construction company. I managed all the administrative tasks. In addition to preparing contracts, proposals, the invoices, overseeing accounts payable and receivable, I spent large amounts of time learning the features of our accounting software and keeping the books. My business partner, on the other hand, was on the golf course, almost every day.

I missed going to lunch with friends because I wanted to get back to work at the office, which I refer to as the *warehouse*. I felt I could save money by doing all the administrative tasks, alone. Keep in mind that our company was rapidly growing as a highly successful firm. At the time, my accountant offered a bookkeeping service for a monthly fee of $100. Imagine that I was not willing to spend a hundred dollars for my CPA to do what his company was professionally licensed to do. Instead of paying him the $100 a month, I did the books myself.

Ironically, one of the reasons we go into business is to have certain freedoms, one of which is we get to be the boss of our schedule. Obviously, I missed the point. Instead of taking advantage of those freedoms, I became a slave to the enterprise and lost what I thought I was saving. This point is critically important as it applies to your business and to your life, in general. We must be mindful that we do not become slaves to what we own. This can happen should we fail to properly steward our time, money, relationships, etc., becoming a servant to what was purposed to serve us. The following seeds shine the light on the collective use of time and energy and their impact on money, whether saved or lost.

1st Seed: Money saved can be an actual loss.

Sometimes what you are saving in money can result in greater losses in several ways. There is a direct relationship between the money you save and your workload. In my case, saving money meant that I would become stressed, overloaded, and less productive. On this continuum, the money that I was saving was far less than the money I would eventually have to spend.

Besides the loss of productivity and personal wellness, I was potentially losing opportunities. Kenneth and Charlene were affluent and well-connected in the community. Their connections to power brokers could have led to a broader clientele base for my company. However, this would require my cultivating a relationship off the tennis court, where our conversations would surpass topics beyond the game of tennis. While I cannot say whether Kenneth and Charlene would have introduced me to their circle of contacts, what I am certain of, however, is that I forfeited the opportunity to find out. My only focus was getting back to the *warehouse*, figuratively. Meanwhile, my business partner was at the golf course, literally.

Adopting the mindset of doing everything singlehandedly was counterproductive in my seeking to build sustainable profits in my business. What I failed to understand was that owning the business did not require me to allow the business to own me. I, myself, did not have to do every task within the business. In my immaturity, I was acting like an employee, a contractor, a temp, a girl Friday—everyone but the owner/CEO. When we think of CEO's, we generally don't envision them inside of a warehouse or even sitting behind a computer all day. We picture them somewhere making bigger deals on golf courses, at business lunches and dinners, on cruises—places that do not look like an office or an administrative space. As for me, I had the CEO title, but lacked the CEO mindset. Therefore, in some instances, I did not manage my time, money, energy, and responsibilities in such a way that ensured the money I was saving far exceeded the cost of what I was losing!

ALICIA D. RITCHEY, Ed.D.

2nd Seed: Time and energy are resources that cannot be equated in dollars and cents.

The value of time and energy is greater than the value of money. As a matter of fact, even though we may give them a certain monetary value, time and energy are rare resources that cannot even be quantified in dollars and cents. Once you have spent the time, it is gone. Once the minutes and hours pass on the clock, you will never see that time again.

Energy, like time, is a resource that is needed to accomplish any work, starting at the conceptual phase, through the execution phase, and whatever comes after that. Some forms of energy include kinetic energy, potential energy, light energy, heat energy, chemical energy, electrical energy, sound energy, etc. Even when just performing a single task, multiple forms of energy are used. With so much energy exerted in the course of a day, how then can we determine its value in monetary terms? While energy may be plentiful, misuse of it, as in overexertion, can be dangerous. Therefore, we must be sure that we are not spending more time and energy than necessary in an attempt to save money on a task we take on to complete ourselves.

Frequently, we see and hear about programs, software, designs, and apps for everything our business needs. Whether it is Canva for graphic design, Dubsado for automating workflows, Mailchimp for email campaigns, and the list goes on. How often have you said to yourself, "Oh, I can do this, or I can do that." While it is true that over time, we can learn all of this and more, the question becomes, how much time and energy will it take for us to build the skills to do all of this with mastery? Would our time and energy be better spent doing what is within our natural gifts and talents, that which comes to us with ease? Going back to the example of Paul, my CPA, and me. Paul and his team do a stellar job preparing taxes, bookkeeping, financial auditing, organizing businesses from A to Z. They understand tax laws, generally acceptable accounting principles, you name it. Not to mention, he is well-versed in Quickbooks, the accounting platform I was using. His bookkeeping staff reconciles accounts every day and could probably do this in their sleep. What would take me hours to complete would only take minutes for Paul and his team. Here I was thinking I was saving when I was spending—spending time that once expended is likely irretrievable, and energy—the resource used in multiple forms.

3rd Seed: Offload everything that is not your zone of core genius.

Often when people start businesses, it is because they realize that they could generate revenue from their hobby or from something they do well, something they feel called to do as part of their life purpose. This might also be called the individual's zone of core genius. Typically, this is the primary craft of the business, the source where most of the revenue is generated. Besides the creation and delivery of products and services, other important elements of the business include sales and marketing, as well as administration and management. Rarely do you find someone who is able to demonstrate mastery, to the same degree, in all three areas of business. With just 24 hours in a day, business owners must determine where they perform best—what area do they demonstrate excellence and passion with efficiency. Trying to stretch themselves across creating the product or service to doing the sales and marketing to administration and management... this is the exact mindset that leads to a path of rapid decline and burnout. This is where business owners are likely to become slaves to their enterprises. This is the point where we must reassess how we manage our entrepreneurial freedoms and ask ourselves, "Have we chosen the *golf course* or have we opted for the *warehouse*?" Quite honestly, if we have spent time working for someone else, it's likely we have already done the warehouse gig. Now as the owner of our business, even if just the business of our lives, we get to choose to offload what is not in our zone of core genius. This does not mean that there are tasks that are beneath us. After all, managing my books was not beneath me. However, my accountant can perform the task better than I, using far less time and far less energy.

One way to determine what tasks to offload is to create a list of all your skills. Now extract from the list those tasks that align with what you believe is your life purpose. Perhaps these tasks fit into the category of your gifts and talents. Whatever is left is likely to be the tasks you should offload or delegate to someone else. Not only will you reduce the risk of burnout, the return on your investment of properly allocated time and energy will yield a fulfilled life, with great pleasure in your work, and other forms of profit.

In summary, the topic of the *golf course* or the *warehouse* is about how we spend our time and energy. Money saved can sometimes be money lost. You can lose it in healthcare expenses and dwindling productivity. You can lose it in missed opportunities. Again, the time and energy you are expending can sometimes be far more valuable than the money that you think you may be saving. The reality is that time and energy are rare resources that cannot even be equated in dollars and cents. Once they have been dispensed, they can hardly be retrieved. We must, therefore, be strategic about how we use our time and our energy. Operating within our zone of core genius must be a part of the strategy. Remember to design your business and your life with allowances for the *golf course*, so you do not, by default, spend all your time inside the *warehouse*. **Take a bite! Enjoy the Slice!**

SLICE 11

OPPORTUNITY OUT OF CRISIS.

One semester, during the time when I was near completion of my coursework for my doctoral degree from Florida International University, I fell behind in paying for my classes. I missed the deadline, and to avoid cancellation of my classes, I went to the Bursar's Office to request an extension. I assumed I would be granted automatic approval since, in the history of my matriculation at the Institution, I had never been late paying for my courses. After speaking with the Supervisor, who could make the final decision, she responded, "You missed the deadline, and we will not be able to grant you an extension."

I pleaded with the woman, but to no avail. I offered her a myriad of reasons why I was delayed with my payment. She still maintained her position of refusal to grant me an extension. After some time of making a pitiful pointless plea, and now becoming emotionally exhausted, I gave it one last shot. You would never imagine what I did. I laid myself down, like a graceful fall, in the middle of the floor in the woman's office and started crying, "My daddy died!" Granted, my dad had passed several years prior to that semester. Yet I reasoned that his passing was the perfect situation to use to my advantage.

The woman replied to my hysteria, "Okay. Please get up. I'll give you the extension."

To seal the deal, I continued, "My daddy died, and all you care about is this money that I owe!"

"Alicia, please get up. Don't do this. I said I'll give you the extension," she begged of me.

Frustrated that it had to get to this point, I cried some more. I determined that she would have to work hard to get me to calm down. I think I cried for every incoming student, who needed her to be more sensitive to their needs, and to be extra supportive of those who had a track record of showing responsibility for making timely payments semester after semester. I thought to myself, "Ma'am, call a film academy because I am going to win an award for this performance."

There were two ladies working in the front office, who saw and heard the entire show. I knew the ladies very well, and I glimpsed them looking at each other in disbelief, as if to say, "Do you believe Alicia is carrying on like that?" They knew my dad's passing was not recent. But, my histrionics served its purpose; I got what I needed, which was the extension.

As I left the building and was walking to my car, the two ladies from the front office were walking to their cars, as well. One of the ladies chuckled and said, "Alicia, I know you did not do that. Your Dad has been dead for years."

"Listen," I replied. "I needed that extension, and my dad really did pass away. She didn't need to know when. I didn't have the money to pay for my classes. The only currency I had in my pocket was the situation around my dad's passing. I had to make it work." As dramatic as it was for me to lay on the floor and start crying, it didn't seem like a bad idea to use what I had.

It's not uncommon that business owners face a financial dilemma and need the extension of time and grace to catch up on bills and other responsibilities. Do not fret. Learn to make the best out of every situation, including the challenge you may be facing. I would even say, "you can lean on the pole of another crisis as support for your existing dilemma." By no means am I saying that you should get on the floor and cry just to make a plea to your creditors. I am suggesting that in every adverse circumstance, there is a pre-dated crisis that can be used to your advantage, whether now or stored for later.

You may not have the courage to present the kind of performance that I did; however, you do well to learn to leverage crises as part of your negotiation strategy to secure opportunity; particularly, in our present economy, where business owners are struggling to stay afloat. Life brings its share of dire experiences, some more traumatic than others. Still, no part of our lives need be wasted. As an example, if you have ever lived in a rural community, you may have seen how farmers package and sell most every part of the hog, wasting nothing (i.e., intestines for chitterlings; the neck for neck bones; the feet, tail, and head for hog head cheese and souse meat; the liver; the brains, hog maw, ears, etc.). What may be unthinkable for consumption for some is tasty to others. The point is, even in the most challenging and difficult seasons, with experiences that are disruptive, traumatic, and egregious—every bit of these crises, though negative in nature, can be used for our benefit and turned for value and profit.

Let's examine my experience to see what seeds are found in this Slice, particularly what strategies business owners can employ during economic crises to keep their doors open and to continue serving their clientele, who depend on their products and services in their daily lives.

1st Seed: Don't be afraid to declare hardship during a crisis.

In reference to my personal experience, I was not trying to avoid paying the University. I merely needed some time to gather the necessary funds to cover the cost of the courses. In that instance, I was pleading my case of a personal hardship. Sometimes, the hardship on a business may be the result of what is happening on a global scale, just as we saw with the Pandemic, and its widespread impact on businesses all over the world.

For those business owners, who took advantage of this world-wide crisis, they were able to secure assistance with meeting payroll, technology upgrades, rental expenses, etc. Of course, not all crises show up to this degree, and neither does support. Obviously, my experience was personal. Just because I was facing hardship did not mean other students were facing the same challenges. Nonetheless, I was able to make my own case for an extension, using the crisis available to me—my father's passing, even though it was outdated. Sometimes we must become good at recycling an old predicament for a present need, making use of a bad circumstance to support an existing cause. Again, this is not to shun responsibility, but to find patience as we transition beyond possible financial hardship and other dilemmas.

Sometimes, our businesses need a break, just as we do on a personal level. The truth of the matter is, creditors understand when we may be facing a crisis, because they are often experiencing similar challenges. So don't be afraid in this hour to declare hardship. Figuratively speaking, get on the floor and scream as you tell your creditors that your business is being challenged right now. Tell them you need an extension. Who knows? This could be the time when you get rid of some unwanted debt, or at least get the debt under control. This could be the time when you gather yourself, refocus, pivot, or just breathe, but you cannot be afraid to declare hardship.

2nd Seed: Old skills can accomplish new work during a crisis.

Given the present economy, some businesses are facing unprecedented risks, including risks related to supply chain, resources, competition, economics, compliance, technology, and the list goes on. You do not have to call it quits despite the grave pressures you may be experiencing. Put on your helmet of wealth—your wealth *brain*. Detect the external risks in the environment and shift as necessary. Remember, in this hour, consumers still have needs to be met, and you are one of the solutions to meet their needs.

Look inside your toolbox to find those old skill sets. You still have them. Dust them off. They still work. Put them to work! This may require you to repackage your skills, or even to repurpose them for this time in history. Sometimes that means shifting from strength to wisdom, from vocation to education. In other words, repackaging your skill set may call you from doing the work in vocation to now training others through education. Or repackaging could be a matter of you rebranding yourself from education to motivation, where you are no longer the person doing the training through education. Now you become the motivation, the person giving keynote speeches on a particular topic.

If there is a need, there is no scarcity of work. Perhaps there is scarcity of ideas, innovation, and invention about how to accomplish the work. All of the necessary tools, however, can be found inside your toolbox. Look again, only this time through the eyes of abundance. Take note of your possessions—your technical and power skills, your expertise, your experience, your connections—all of which can be monetized and can position you as an invaluable resource. Prepare yourself for a relaunch, stronger and better than before.

3rd **Seed: A crisis precedes new normalcy.**

As we witnessed during the Pandemic, we have entered the space of a new normal. People are developing new habits. Their needs and desires are changing, all due to the Covid-19 crisis.

Who would think that online celebrations would take off the way it did since 2020? DJs were throwing live on-line parties with attendance numbers of over 10,000 people in what they called cyber clubs. What this showed us is, in this new normal, you can reach people who would otherwise never have been accessible to you. You can get your products and services to people in innovative new ways.

From the crisis of the Pandemic, which ushered in this new normalcy, we learned to become more comfortable with change, seeing that this is not the era of business as usual. Look at the ways in which the world has shifted in the last two years. Given the rapid speed of change in our society, continuous growth and development must be a constant in our businesses. Do yourself a favor. Take an assessment of where you are in your business. Then determine where you need to be in order to strive. With the shift taking place in our society right before our eyes, you must be ready, and stay ready, or get left behind!

In summary, a crisis can bring about opportunities that work to benefit you and your business. Learn to integrate crises into your negotiation strategy for favorable outcomes, whether you are experiencing a major decline in your revenue, a decline in production, or other concerns. Don't overlook an aged toolbox. It's a treasure trove. When you look through the lens of wealth, you will discover fresh ideas and inventions that provide solutions to current consumer needs. Ask yourself, "Am I an education resource?" An entertainment resource, maybe? Are you a financial resource? What about a culinary resource? As a resource, you not only solve other people's problems, but you are also a supply chain of wealth and revenue for your own perpetual sustainability. Lastly, let growth be a constant within your business operation. In this way, you are more likely prepared for the new normal, in whatever form it presents itself. **Take a bite! Enjoy the Slice!**

SLICE 12

PREPARING FOR TIME AND CHANCE.

Around January of 2018, I received a call from someone asking if I could develop a curriculum for a course they were preparing to teach. When I responded that I could, they asked for a price. After I gave the cost of my service, I never heard back from the person again. Quite honestly, it was the first time I had been asked to develop a curriculum for an individual business owner. Having a background in curriculum and instruction, I knew I could deliver on my promise to provide a high-quality product; however, I was not as prepared to start the inquirer on a client journey. From that experience, I made myself ready by developing a questionnaire, in case I was ever asked by someone else to develop a curriculum.

A few weeks later, after creating my questionnaire, I was recommended by a business coach to write social media ads for

ALICIA D. RITCHEY, Ed.D.

another business owner. The business owner later called me to discuss her interest. When she asked if I write social media ads, I replied, "Absolutely. I write social media ads with no problem," even though before this time, I had never been asked to write social media ads. Knowing what service she needed prior to the call, I researched the market value of that service, and could speak quite confidently about how I could deliver to exceed her expectation. After I gave her the cost of my service, she shared that she was hoping to begin her project sometime in February of that year, just weeks away from the date of the phone call. I never heard from her again.

With the two inquiries for two different services—curriculum development and copy writing for social media ads—I was prompted to develop a fee schedule. On the fee schedule, I had costs for my services of curriculum development, social media ads, and other types of written content commonly requested by business owners. I was building, based on the perceived demand. In addition to the fee schedule, I also created workflows, forms, and standardized emails to onboard new clients for a smooth customer journey. I knew I was preparing for something big, though I was not exactly sure what it was.

You probably guessed that a few weeks later, I received another phone call, this time from someone who wanted a content writer for her website. I assured her I could provide the services she requested. When she asked for a proposal, I developed the proposal, and I sent it to her. While I never heard from her again, I did not get discouraged. In fact, I simply added to the fee schedule the cost of service for writing content for website pages. Nothing was lost. With each inquiry, I educated myself by conducting further research on what I could command as a professional writer. Added to my portfolio of a broad range of writing services, I was getting more comfortable with stating the cost of my service and the value of my offer.

Soon after, I received another call from a woman who had just started a credit repair company. This was the chance I had been waiting for. Guess what? She wanted and accepted many of the services the prior individuals only inquired about without accepting my offer. I was ready for her. Not only had I used my time to prepare a questionnaire, my fee schedule, and other onboarding essentials, but I also used the previous inquiries as a springboard to practice articulating my value. Now let's see what seeds we can share about the value of time in preparing for the chance that awaits you.

1st Seed: Don't chase chance. Prepare for it!

Believe it or not, the chance at big opportunities is headed in your direction. In fact, big opportunities will not only come towards you, but they will also chase after you. So, the question becomes, "If I don't have to chase after opportunities, what do I do until they arrive?" The answer is simple, "prepare." This takes us back to our strategic use of time—the resource you are given to prepare for your chance at big opportunities you may be hoping for.

Let's think about the series of phone calls I received before a major opportunity appeared. With the first call, the woman inquired about my service for curriculum development for a course she wanted to offer. While I did not land the client, her inquiry prompted me to develop a questionnaire that I could use for future clients. With the questionnaire, the process of onboarding future clients would be a lot easier.

The second phone caller was a woman who inquired as to whether I could write social media ads. Like the first caller, she wasn't that big chance, but she was an indicator that chance was on the horizon. So, what did I do when I did not land her as a client? I developed a fee schedule. In that way, if other potential clients were to ask me about my services for writing social media ads, I would have a fee schedule available. Now I've got a questionnaire for someone who wants me to develop course curriculum. I also have a fee schedule. I even developed a proposal for new clients, a welcome packet, forms, and workflows.

Before my big opportunity appeared, a third caller showed up wanting content for her website. Although she never secured my services, I was more prepared than before to engage her in conversation around what I could provide. This was all a part of the rehearsal. While I never again heard from any of the three persons, each phone call was part of a composite of what was coming. I could see that chance was brewing, and I was using my time to prepare for it. Neither of the three personified chance. However, they were instrumental in my preparation, and helped me identify key points in the process.

2nd Seed: Shine. Don't grind! To "go consistent" is better than to "go hard."

It is common these days to hear people profess to be on their grind. When I think of grind, however, I think of two forces working in opposition to each other, where one of them will give way. And that one is usually you, the business owner. Envision yourself constantly grinding or pounding on a sidewalk. While it is not likely that the sidewalk will move, by the time you reach the sidewalk's end, you would have sacrificed your joints, like bone on bone. The same applies in business, which could be styled as the sidewalk. The business may yet be standing and intact; however, like the instance of you pounding the sidewalk; when you are in constant grind mode, you are giving way in your clarity, focus, productivity, strength, relationships, mental health, and your overall well-being.

Grind is born out of hustle culture. The two—hustle and grind—work together reducing optimal productivity in ways that negatively impacts your bottom line. If anybody knows me, they know I am opposed to hustle culture, particularly as a mode of management for a business operation. Hustle as a business design is rooted in constant hard work. Defined in this way, hustle lacks strategy, systems, self-care, and long-term sustainability. Hustle, seen in this light, is a flawed, unfinished, imposturous operation, perpetrating as a legitimate business. Grind then is how this type operation is managed, and how one executes the tasks within the operation.

On the other hand, to shine means that you and all aspects of your business are working in harmony. You and your sales and marketing strategy; you and your administration and management; you and your products and services; you and your revenue; you and your team—all things are operating like a well-oiled machine. Why then should you grind when you can shine?!

3rd Seed: Add pace to preparation for a smooth finish and a polished look.

Pace is a secret sauce. It is like a finishing touch, a polished look of swag. Have you ever noticed a well-dressed gentleman wearing a classic suit? When we describe him as having swag, we are often referring to his style of walking. There is something about the timing of his steps and the way he lays his feet at a certain tempo that is rhythmic and smooth. If the same gentleman, wearing the same outfit, were to start running, his swag would not be as pronounced. However, if he slows down and begins to walk in a deliberately moderate pace as before, we might say he has recovered his swag. This is the difference that pace can make as you prepare and wait for chance, which we know is on its way.

Pace is not about slowing down the process, it is about being intentional to avoid burnout, so that when chance arrives, you have the necessary strength and stamina to take advantage of the opportunity. With pace, we take full advantage of not only the opportunity of chance, but we also take advantage of what the journey provides us, as well. For instance, think of a great book you have read, perhaps an autobiography of someone's life. While the story of the person's life may interest you as a relatable text, it's the lessons you can draw from their life that really add benefit to you. When you don't situate pace inside of time, then you run past the lessons. And without the lessons, the experience has no value.

Another advantage of pace is that it allows you to stop to smell the roses. When you forego time and do not adjust your pace to smell the roses, you forfeit the beauty of life. Can you imagine a life lived without regard for the beauty of it? Additionally, pace provides you with opportunities to cultivate relationships. Let's say you have the task of pushing down a wall in an old building. To get to the wall, you walk down a long corridor, where there are people on both sides of the hallway. You pass the people and fail to acknowledge their presence. You're moving swiftly down the hall without pacing yourself. You only have the task in mind! Clearly, you have not built a relationship with the people you are passing. Finally, you reach the wall, and realize that you need help because it is impossible to push down the wall alone. You look back at the people you have passed, and no one is moving to assist you. Had you been more intentional about how you used pace to prepare for your chance to push down the wall, you would have help in your time of need. With proper pace, you give yourself the time to cultivate relationships such that when you get to challenging tasks, you have allies to help you accomplish them.

In summary, do not chase chance. Allow your chance to come running after you. This is a fact of life! Chance comes to everyone. Everyone will get their chance. The question becomes, "Have you used time to prepare for it?" You don't have to "go hard." Remember the sidewalk is concrete; likely, it's not going to move. Therefore, instead of choosing to "go hard," just "go consistent." There is no need to grind when you can simply shine! And finally, incorporate pace with time as part of the strategy you use to prepare for chance. With pace, you are being consistent and intentional, and at the end of the day, much is accomplished—great milestones and great rewards. **Take a bite! Enjoy the Slice!**

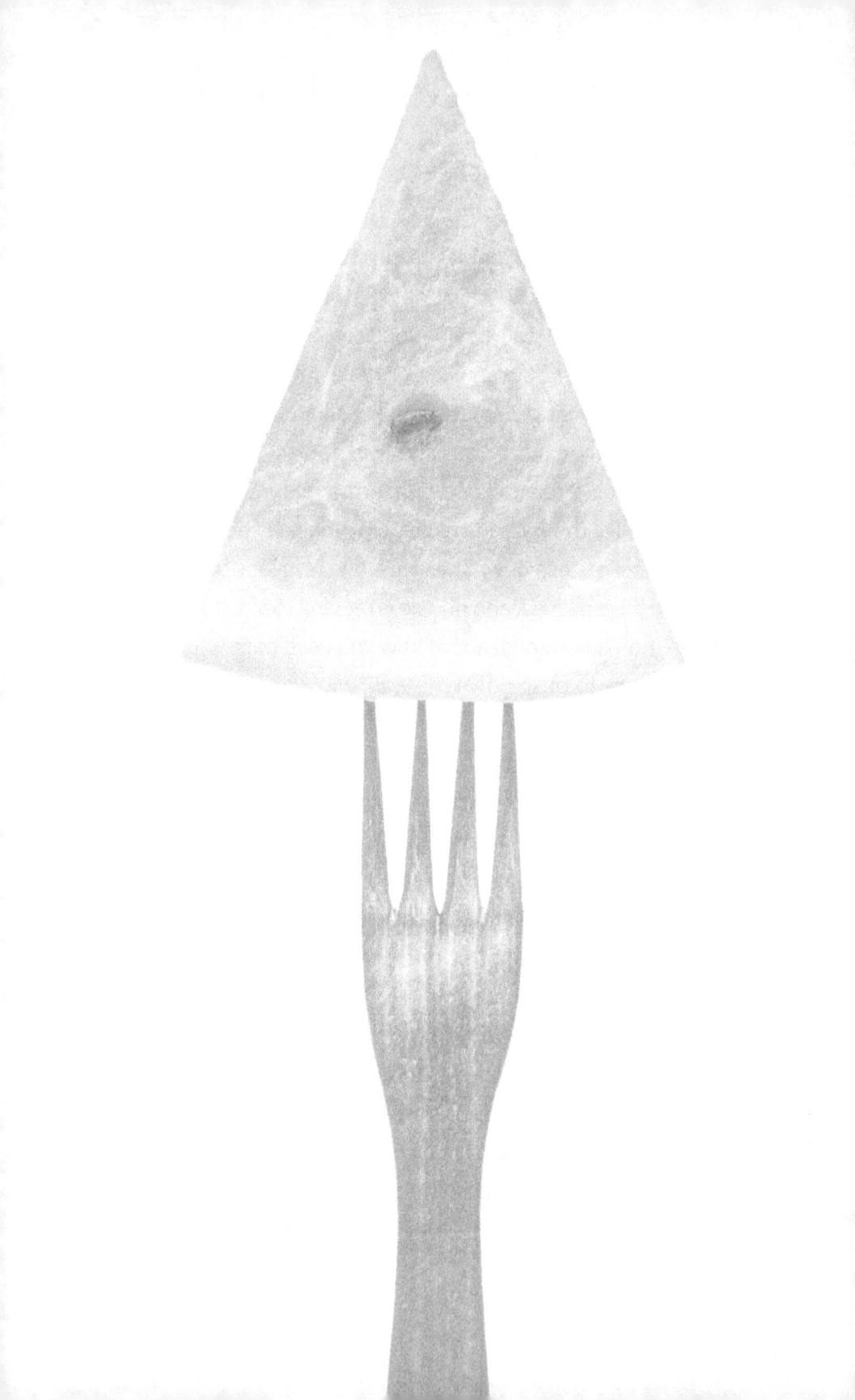

SLICE 13

SHARE THE GIFT. WALK IN PURPOSE.

You have likely heard the idiom, "the gift that keeps on giving." In this Slice, we are revisiting our gifts and how they show up in our business and in our everyday lives. My intention here is to encourage business owners to understand how entrepreneurship should be a spiritual journey of self-discovery and growth. As well, it is a journey of us bringing light to our communities through our shared gifts: a display of beauty, creativity, innovation, and excellence expressed in the form of products and services we provide.

We begin our discussion making a case that business ownership, when viewed through spiritual lens, is an answer to a divine calling to improve the human condition with our gifts. We continue our discussion showing the importance of sharing our gifts, how this impacts others, and how value is added through positive responses to our gifts. We also examine the power of **being** versus **doing**, and the role this plays as business owners use their resources to enhance opportunities for them to share their gifts. We conclude our discussion around the thought that while business owners should be intentional to reach the masses with their gifts, sometimes there may be a difference between the immense value of the gift and the monetary value you can garner through this exchange, which may vary depending on the demographic you are called to serve. I make a point to highlight how the idea of **difference** can work in your favor as others continue to be inspired by our gifts—gifts that keep on giving.

1st Seed: Sharing our gifts is how we answer our divine calling.

Often, people do not see entrepreneurship as the answer to a divine calling or fulfillment of life purpose. Perhaps this is because entrepreneurialism is known to be a form of capitalism, with the motive of making a profit. I should make it clear, however, that I am approaching this discussion of entrepreneurship or private enterprise from the vein of purpose work, where gifts are born out of a spiritual calling, yet can be monetized for profit, though not from a place of greed, extortion, deceit, or negative conflict—but toward the fulfillment of purpose. The business entity is merely the structure where the gift is housed and managed. Through our business activity, we can reach the masses—those who will affirm the value of our gifts—those who buy it and those who buy into it. That includes any stakeholder, whether a client, employee, volunteer, or even competitor. When we distribute our gifts to the masses, we have a unique opportunity to improve the quality of life for those who heed the call as consumers of the gift. If that is the purpose of the gift, why then would we withhold it from some? After all, the more hands in which your gifts are found, the more you fulfill your life purpose. And again, if people buy it or buy into it, they are making an open declaration that your gifts have great value. In business, we might call that a testimonial.

The more value that is ascribed to our gifts, the more inclined we become to share, and to share with passion. Passion is like oil that causes our talents to ooze from us, without even trying. I warn that passion must be managed, so that our gifts do not exhaust the receiver, overwork the giver, and flow in such excess that it becomes waste. Therefore, passion must be accompanied with temperance for an even spread so that you, the giver, can operate in balance and continue answering the divine call.

2nd Seed: Your "being" is more productive than your doing.

In a spiritual sense, entrepreneurship is more than making a profit from our gifts. If profit alone is what motivates you in business, then you may be willing to profit at the expense of others. On a higher human level, entrepreneurship also involves strategic use of resources to propel gifts into the hands of the masses, where profit is not the ultimate goal of pursuit. Instead, it is the by-product of fulfilling one's life purpose. Seen in this light, money and other forms of profit are outcomes of who we are, the state of our *being*, not just what we visibly and tangibly produce.

I make the distinction between *being* and *doing* to show how each has its unique outcome. Your *being* relates to the quality of your present state. It stands to reason then, that one's present state may vary depending on the current situation. However, even when the circumstance changes, people tend to be consistent in their responses to the situation, no matter what it is. Think about it. When people are naturally happy, except in the instance of a gravely traumatic experience, their happy state of *being* remains fairly consistent throughout the course of their lives. The same can be said about people who are pessimistic. From situation to situation, they tend to have a gloomy outlook on life, even when the situation appears hopeful to another. We should understand that your *being* relates also to your attitude, your outlook (in terms of how you see yourself and others), your worldview, and the values you adopt as principles by which to live. Over time, your *being* becomes your known identity.

As I mentioned, the term *being* relates to attitude and intention. Therefore, for purposes of this discussion, I use the terms attitude and state of *being* interchangeably. Your attitude is expressed through your behaviors, whether positive or negative. Individuals can sometimes mask their attitudes and intentions; however, these are made known by their behaviors. Behaviors become the vehicle which your attitude uses to communicate its state or position in ways that others can read, interpret, evaluate, and make responses to. This is why I say, your *being* is a more dominant force than your *doing*. In fact, your *being* is the precursor to your doing, which can be seen as a visible or tangible outcome that is prompted and instructed by your *being*. Said another way, perhaps more simply put, your behaviors are guided by your attitude.

Behaviors are not only the outcomes of products and services you provide, but also how you engage with your clientele and other stakeholders. Repeated behaviors communicate messages of one's intention to include or exclude, to empower or disenfranchise, to value or devalue, to foster community or division. All of this is important because your *being* also dictates how you show up in your business and in your everyday life. Your attitude and intentions—the nature of your being—cannot be separated from what you put out or produce.

I think of my decades of experience as a classroom educator, as an example. The attitude (state of *being*, character, and values) of the teacher is expressed at every stage of the instructional process, from planning to instructional delivery to assessment to classroom management. If the teacher's state of *being* is negative, others detect it—perhaps through the curricular choices the teacher makes, types of assessment the teacher uses, the student-teacher interactions, the teachers' exclusion or inclusion of certain groups of students, or how the teacher manages conflict. The attitude or *being* of the teacher will shine through. For certain, students, as well as parents, will know it. So will the school-site administration, as well as the district. Look at the power of the teacher's *being* (attitude) and what it produces—a certain instructional quality, classroom social climate, student responses by way of their academic performance (learning gains and rates of passing, as well as grade-level retention and matriculation), not to mention the impact this has on families and communities.

ALICIA D. RITCHEY, Ed.D.

When and if we consider who we are as business owners, we can make meaningful assessments about the quality of the products and services we provide simply by examining our *being*. Given the right attitude, our products can have a positive impact on end users. Using the example of classroom teachers, whose attitudes or states of *being* is reflected in all aspects of their instructional practice, the same applies for business owners and their observable tangible products, known as products and services. Their selection of materials and ingredients that go into a product, how the product is manufactured, the process used in delivering to the customer, the customer experience, and the value you promise to the customer—all of this is a direct outcome of business owners' state of being, in addition to their attitude toward certain demographics and communities.

If business owners' *being* or attitude influences the quality of their products and services, then we can also see the affect this has on the business brand and profitability. As earlier implied, a positive state of *being* or attitude creates products that positively affects the client. The client then interprets that the product is a result of the business owner's positive state of *being* or attitude toward certain groups. Taken together, the product, along with the clients' experiences and perceptions around the product, creates a brand that is fossilized into public opinion.

You probably can think of several instances where there have been public outcries against the use of certain products. In these instances, corporations are forced to spend exorbitant amounts of money in their efforts to recover their brands from negative media coverage, boycotting, and class action lawsuits. The series of complaints are targeted more at the state of *being* of the business owner and their attitude toward certain demographics. The quality of the product is measured by the impact this has on various sects of society. Again, our *being* communicates certain values that take the form of a product or service. The product or service can be traced back to the nature of our *being* or our attitude and our intentions, whether to benefit certain groups or not. This says that as business owners, our business brands and long-term profitability requires that we take stock of our character, evaluate our attitudes, ensure wellness for our inner *being*, so that our products and services show up in the marketplace in ways that positively contribute to the good of humankind.

3rd Seed: Make the difference work for you.

To cultivate this seed, let's use the example of homeownership. If you have ever owned a house or a building of any type, then you probably know that the house (or building) has a determined assessed value. This amount may be different from the amount you owe to the lender who financed the property. The difference between the two figures is called equity. For example, your house may be valued at $100,000. If you have a balance of $30,000 due to the lender for the property, then the positive difference of $70,000 is what we call equity (borrowing power or money available to the owner), which can be used at the owner's discretion. You can do a lot with $70,000 of equity.

ALICIA D. RITCHEY, Ed.D.

You may choose to use that money as a down payment on another property. You may choose to use a part of the $70,000 difference to make upgrades to your existing property, or even as capital to start or expand a business. Perhaps, you may decide not to touch your equity; instead, you may allow it to continue growing until you fully pay off the mortgage on the property. In whatever way you choose to use it, equity is available to you. And that equity can work for you.

The point of this seed is not really to discuss equity. The primary focus is to illustrate the power of *difference*, which can be used to your advantage, depending on the term you use to describe it and justify it. In a social science context, sadly, *difference* from the mainstream has often been used to disenfranchise others, who are considered to be outside the norm, where because of their *difference*, they are falsely viewed as inherently inferior. In so doing, the value and contributions of entire sects of people become invalidated, which in turn, impedes the progress of humanity.

Similarly, in business, sometimes entrepreneurs do not view difference for the value it adds. Consequently, money is left on the table. In the example of the house, *difference* was termed as equity, which the homeowner can use to access cash at will. Earlier in the book (See Slice #2, 2nd seed), I mentioned the term product differentiation to describe *difference* as your uniqueness—how you stand out from your competitors. In the following section, I will discuss another type of *difference,* more commonly termed as *loss*. We don't often think of *loss* in a positive light. Nonetheless, like the other forms of *difference* I mentioned, depending on how you treat, classify, or term the *loss*, you can still find gains around the *loss* and recoup the *difference* in other ways, as you share your gift.

So how does the example of a house, its assessed value, outstanding balances, and equity relate to your business? More specifically, what does all this have to do with you sharing your gifts within your business? To answer the questions, we begin by looking at certain figures related to your business sales as we did with the prior example of the house. Consider that the assessed value of your product or service has one dollar amount. Then you also have the amount your client is willing to pay you for the product or service. Often, there is a difference between these two figures, which can be another dollar amount. Using the same dollar values from the example of the house, we might say the assessed value of the product is $100,000. The client may be willing to pay you only $30,000. The difference being $70,000. My question to you is what do we do with the difference between these two figures?

In business, this difference is not called equity. Clearly, this would be considered a loss. With this kind of loss, the business owner is likely to become reluctant to engage in future transactions of this kind. Be warned, once you perceive the *difference* as a *loss*, then not only are you giving away your entrepreneurial power (See Slice 3). This could also impact your willingness to share the gift, and consequently diminish its value. Remember, each time someone buys [or buys into] your gift, expressed as your product or service, value is added.

ALICIA D. RITCHEY, Ed.D.

While I don't suggest you make it a normal business practice to just give away your gifts without expectation of a monetary return, what I will tell you is that when you find yourself facing these outcomes, you can make the ***difference*** work for you. In the instance of the house, the figure difference of $70,000 was called equity. I mentioned that people use the ***difference,*** or the equity, however they choose. Likewise, as a business owner, you get to name your ***difference*** or seeming loss, however you choose, depending on your business needs.

You may choose to consider the *loss* a humanitarian effort, philanthropy, social responsibility, or charitable donation. Perhaps you name your *loss* as bad debt, or a discount to the client. However you choose to name the loss (the difference between the assessed value of your product or service and the amount your client is willing to pay you for it), make the difference work for you. As a gain to your business, seek advice from a tax professional for assistance with properly naming the transaction, so that the *loss* can be written off on your taxes and reflected on your financial statements.

Why is it important that we have this discussion about how you classify this ***difference*** or ***loss***? It is because, if we view entrepreneurship as our life purpose, then that purpose may lead us to operate our business in places where $100,000, or any six figure amount, is not even attainable for the clients you serve. Depending on your life purpose, you may not be assigned to a wealthy class who may be able to say, without blinking an eye, "Here is $100,000 for your product." Sometimes you are assigned to poor people in distressed or under-resourced, communities.

What if purpose takes you to an elderly population, who may be on a fixed income? Sometimes purpose will assign you to people who don't even appreciate the value of what you have. Keep in mind that just because they cannot buy it doesn't mean they will not buy into it. And just because they didn't pay the $100,000, that doesn't diminish the value of the gift. Going in, you already know the value of the gift, but sometimes you are assigned to people who can't afford that value. Well, make the difference work for you.

Remember, the purpose of the gift is to be shared. It is your responsibility to ensure that the gift reaches as many people as possible since it is designed to improve the quality of life of those to whom you are assigned. Again, in the case of a house, the difference between value and what you owe is called equity. As a business owner, you must treat your seeming losses like positive equity, where equity is currency. We make equity, as a form of difference, work for us. As well, you must become astute enough in conducting your business to make all forms of **difference** work for you. Once you understand this principle, then profit is gain and *loss* is gain—a definite win-win!

The notion of finding gains in loss is seen all the time in marketing. The gift may be shared as a promotional item and given away at no cost to the client. The promotional item has a monetary value, yet it is given away with no expectation of payment from the client. This difference, however, is recouped in brand awareness or future sales. Another example is when music artists perform in the Super Bowl®. They may not be compensated for their performance, but their association with a mega brand gives them massive media exposure. Now their clientele base expands exponentially, and their sales skyrocket into the stratosphere. The difference can be recouped in written or video testimonials. **Difference** may be recouped in bartering opportunities, future speaking engagements, endorsements, shared contact information for more leads, letters of acknowledgment, recommendations, as well as opportunities to test the product and conduct market research.

In summary, when we share our gifts, and people buy into our gifts, the value of the gifts is affirmed. Then we are walking in our purpose. Our gifts are important for use—to improve the quality of life of every person who experiences it, whether through purchase or simply admiring from afar. During the transaction of sharing our gifts, we hope to net a profit. However, in the event you receive less than the value of what you determine the gift is worth, make the *difference* work for you. This *difference* does not have to equate to a loss with no gain. Define the *difference* such that you can recoup the loss and receive greater wins in other ways. Finally, our gifts are a display of beauty, creativity, innovation, and excellence expressed in the form of the products and services we provide. Share the gift! Walk in purpose, and watch how you profit in your overall life! ***Take a bite! Enjoy the Slice!***

SLICE 14

GET YOUR OWN DICTIONARY.

A few years ago, I was in an accountability group of five women—four wonderful sister-friends and myself. We committed to keeping each other encouraged to continue working on our businesses during the Pandemic. One week, I was not feeling well and was confined to bed rest. Each day, the ladies posted their accomplishments, and they seemed to be achieving milestones at phenomenal speed. I could not help but notice the high level of productivity they were reporting. Meanwhile, I was in bed, seemingly getting nothing done. You can imagine that little whisper in my ears telling me that I should be doing more than just lying down, despite my obvious need to take some time off to rest.

Besides not feeling well, the idea of being left behind by my four sister-friends did not make me feel any better. The thoughts came swirling: "Aren't you going to jump in and post something? I mean really, what have you done this week? Why are you being unproductive, doing nothing while everybody else is making exceptional strides?"

Have you ever had that experience, where it looks like others around you are completing everything; meanwhile, you're seemingly doing nothing? Personally, I was defining my productivity based on the accomplishments of others. As I pondered further, it dawned on me that when you define what you are doing compared to what others are doing, of course, you run the risk of thinking that you're doing nothing while everybody else is getting all the things done.

At that moment, I thought to myself, "Just one minute! With my own dictionary, I can define productivity in a way that works for me and my personal life." This does not mean that I cannot recognize the success of others. At the same time, however, I can still celebrate my own milestones, even if I am resting in bed. After all, resting is important too.

The following three seeds stress the importance of getting your own dictionary, so you do not make the mistake of defining your success by what others are accomplishing. After examining these seeds, you will be encouraged to forget trying to put your name next to what others are producing and thinking that you must do the same.

1st Seed: Motivation does not require duplication.

Sometimes people will see what someone else is doing and say, "If she launched a book, now I must launch a new book. If he gets a new client, now I must get the same client. If she creates a new product, now I must create that product."

You may be looking at others' online programs, their numbers on social media, even the opportunities they secure, and using all this to measure your productivity and efficiency. We must avoid looking at the attainments of others, perceiving that we should be doing the very same thing. Otherwise, we may be taken completely off the path of our own life purpose and derailed from what we should be accomplishing in our own businesses.

Sure. We can observe what others are doing and be motivated by their performance. Afterall, sometimes by witnessing the achievements of others, we can boost our own level of excellence and become inspired to reach our full potential, however that applies to you. Again, get your own dictionary. Determine how productivity is best defined for you and manifest that, without focusing on how others define success in their glossary of terms.

2nd Seed: Being still can be just as productive as being in motion.

Think about what happens when we are still and at rest, or asleep. We are being refreshed and rejuvenated. The body is able to recuperate from hours of labor. In a state of rest, the body is replenished and refueled with energy. The cells, tissues, and muscles are repaired. Therefore, sometimes we just need to stop and be still, like pause and chill, and allow rest to do its job.

At the highest sleep cycle, known as REM, dreams and visions occur. Ah, imagine that! When one is at rest, now the individual is able to experience visions or dreams. Follow me on this one. I mentioned dreams and visions to make a connection between getting rest and reaching your business goals. Keep in mind that dreams and visions are not only images that we see while asleep. Dreams and visions are also related to personal and professional goals and aspirations that you have for yourself, your business, and otherwise. You might dream of one day becoming a seven or eight figure business owner with a global brand that impacts and transforms communities around the world. With this dream, you will likely find yourself more motivated to stretch higher in order to reach such a lofty goal.

If in a traditional sense, to dream requires that you are at a particular stage of rest, then rest is critical even in achieving your goals since people are inspired through their dreams. This being the case, then rest is not only for rejuvenation, it's also for inspiration. First rest. Next, relax. Then dream while at rest. In a state of rest, it would not be unthinkable to imagine your personal and professional success. Neither would it be unthinkable to imagine yourself as a resource of hope and an influencer within your community and abroad. The dream (what you envision or imagine) inspires you to reach for success. Perhaps people lack inspiration because there is no dream or vision of prosperity. The absence of the dream could be due to constant movement when one should simply be resting.

3rd Seed: To know the value of the process, examine the value of the outcome.

My Dad used to often say, "The end justifies the means." What he meant was that the outcome validates the process. The value of the method is determined by the product it yields.

Going back to the example of rest, my productivity skyrocketed after I rested. We can then say that the outcome of the rest determined that the rest had great value.

Clearly, I needed rest at that season of my life. What would have happened if I had continued to go and go and go, trying to be productive? Not only would I have compromised my mental and physical well-being, but in my persistence, I may likely have given rise to what is referred to as the principle of diminishing return. This means that while working, in a state of fatigue, instead of adding to my productivity, I would be taking from it.

In summary, I encourage you to get your own dictionary! Considering what others are doing may help to motivate you in your own endeavors. However, it is not always necessary that you duplicate what they are doing with the same exactness, expecting that the outcome looks identical to what they produce. Additionally, we must understand that productivity carries as much value in moments of rest as it does in active movement. When I consider my time of the rest, the outcome of the rest was clarity and greater focus, resulting in higher productivity and profitability. I could then determine the value of my getting rest by what I could produce when I arose from sleeping.

Remember, you are the entrepreneur. You have the power to own. So, own your power. Whatever you own, you can also name. Whatever you name, you can also define. After all, the dictionary belongs to you! **Take a bite! Enjoy the Slice!**

"Watermelon never tasted so good.
Take a bite! Enjoy the Slice!"

—Ozzie Ritchey Palmer

WHO WANTS WATERMELON FOR BREAKFAST?

Business lessons to profit your everyday life

ALICIA D. RITCHEY, Ed.D.

ACKNOWLEDGEMENTS

I have been blessed to have the support of many individuals in completing this book project. I must acknowledge that it has meant a great deal to have them in my corner to bring this work to fruition.

To Dexter Hunt, thank you for being my brother and true friend. Your unwavering commitment to the design and layout of this work has brought me to this point of manifestation, "It is finished." I could not have done this without you.

To my teammates and advisors: Dudley Carter, Deryl Hunt II, Genevieve Cave-Hunt, Crystal Harvey, Eneka Ferguson, Dr. Karen Lundy, and Barbara Williams, thank you for listening to my loooooong weekly stories about the concepts shared in the book. Having you present with me on this journey gave me the courage to launch with confidence.

I must acknowledge my bonus Dad, James Palmer, who allowed me countless hours of shared time with my mom to confirm the events around her experiences, to validate the practical use of the concepts in the book, and to share in my excitement the closer we got to the finish line.

Thank you, Lynette Hepburn Richardson, my loyal friend and dedicated publishing administrator, who helped to guide this project and to remind me that there is a story inside each of us. Thank you, to my graphic designer, Melvin McClanahan, for your beautiful cover design, and to you, Belinda Vickerson for your creative eye to capture the essence of my personality in photographic form.

I am grateful to my stellar editing team: Linda Barnes, the MBA on deck, as well as the literary doctors: Dr. Sharon Samuels and Dr. Wendy Wilson. With your academic prowess, professional knowledge, and business acumen, the readers can be assured a clear understanding of the ideas conveyed in this text.

Thank you to my life-long friend, Charlie D. Darrington, who personally witnessed the negative portrayal of the watermelon in the South, yet encouraged me to restore the narrative around this fruit to one of sweet optimism and profitability.

Dr. Sheva Quinn, who pushed me to complete this project many years ago; here we are, Sis Doc! Thank you for providing the Foreword and for being an inspiration of excellence.

Thank you to my brothers, Nick, Dwight and David, my sister, Robin and my nieces, Jordan and Mycah, who engaged me in critical dialogue about particular sections of the book in preparation for the defense of its content and benefit to modern society.

Finally, my gratitude goes out to the two most influential men in my life. First, my biological Dad and hero, David Ritchey, Sr., whose entrepreneurial journey gave me a bird's-eye view of the challenges and rewards of business ownership; and provided me a competitive edge as a fledgling entrepreneur. Secondly, my business mentor emeritus, Dr. Deryl G. Hunt, who convinced me of my calling and position as a 21st Century business leader, and who taught me to understand the world from an interdisciplinary perspective, hence the intersection between my diverse background in education, business, and everyday life.

ABOUT DR. ALICIA RITCHEY

Dr. Alicia D. Ritchey is a premier consultant with expertise in program and curriculum development, professional writing, and senior executive training. She is a product of entrepreneurial heritage. Both her parents owned businesses. Ritchey received her doctorate in Curriculum & Instruction, English Education from Florida International University in Miami, Florida.

A National Board-Certified Teacher, the highest commendation for educators throughout the U.S., Ritchey held numerous posts with Miami-Dade County Public Schools, including instructor, writing coach, and professional development facilitator. She has done international education consulting for governments of the Bahamas, as well as the Turks and Caicos Island.

In 2013, she launched A Ritch Enterprise in Cordele, Georgia. As the first and only federally certified woman-owned small business in Crisp County, her company provides solutions for building organizational capacity through education support, Diversity, Equity, Inclusion training, program design, and business coaching.

For more than two decades, Ritchey has served as senior executive consultant for ICB Productions, Inc., a global training, consulting, and management firm. There she spearheads in the development of training programs and diversity equity and inclusion (DEI) curricula for use within public and private sectors. Given her long-standing affiliation with the firm, Ritchey is celebrated as a leading expert in DEI and inclusive community building affairs.

Dr. Alicia D. Ritchey—a progressive educator, consultant, and trainer, whose innovative and creative engagement practices have positioned her as one of the nation's top 21st Century leaders.

"If people can make money in their sleep, imagine what you can make when you're woke."

—David Ritchey Sr.

"Why opt for a shack of misconception when you can have a mansion of clarity?"

—Deryl G. Hunt, Ph.D.

www.ingramcontent.com/pod-product-compliance
Lightning Source LLC
Chambersburg PA
CBHW021410290426
44108CB00010B/473